Beyond The Shadows:

A Field Guide to the Paranormal

By: Brandon Hudgens and Dennis W. Carroll

Paroline Publishing

Cover photo by Brandon Hudgens
Cover design by Brandon Hudgens and Dennis W. Carroll
Book design by Brandon Hudgens and Dennis W. Carroll

ISBN: 978-0-9898020-1-7
First Printing: August 2013

For those who are brave enough to venture forward in search of the unknown!

Contents

I will tell you this; it takes a certain special kind of person who will leave the warmth and safety of home and with flashlight in hand, go wandering in God forsaken places in the dead hours of night, where few would venture, to walk into the windswept darkness and navigate through ancient ruins and abandoned buildings, and to explore graveyards, deserted houses and the shadowed places of the Earth. Searching, always searching, for the truth. Yes, you never know what you may encounter when you go face to face with the mysteries of this world and dare to shake hands, with the unknown…

Forward

We within the field of exploring the supernatural will more than likely be introduced to this due to an encounter in our younger years. Brandon and Dennis are no exception and this can lead to a calling within the field which grows to such an extent it cannot be ignored.

Both authors describe their early encounters which many of us can relate to, on many levels, but for those that get involved further with the field there is little guidance even at a basic level on the various types of pitfalls within the field.

This book is a perfect guide to get you started, to develop and to grow within the field safely and with enough background to give the amateur a greater grounding giving the new researcher an understanding which will carry them throughout the United States.

Barry Fitzgerald

∞ Beyond the Shadows ∞

"Mystery creates wonder, and wonder is the basis for man's desire to understand. Who knows what mysteries will be solved in our lifetime and what new riddles will become the challenge of the new generations."

John Keel

Preface

Paranormal Research - True Paranormal Research, is and always will be a scientific endeavor. Paranormal research organizations should not exist to be social groups or clubs. They should only be formed with the intent to help and assist people, when they encounter something beyond their normal capacity to deal with in their lives, and of course to gather and assimilate knowledge. This is the basis of all true science, to further the knowledge of mankind, in essence to broaden our horizons as a species.

With the acquisition of such wisdom to our science, we can only better ourselves and gain power to a certain degree over our own destiny. We must research and investigate with all scientific means at our disposal and its criteria must be followed to bring about a sound conclusion to its end. If we fail to do this, it will defeat us in our goals. We must adhere to the rules of genuine science and research in our investigations at all times. Now this is not to say that we shouldn't band together. On the contrary, communication and the exchange of data, research studies and information is a must. Without the transference of ideas and support, we would lose a very valuable asset. But we should always examine ourselves in our research as to what our true and basic motives are - fun and games - or the noble quest for knowledge in our field. This of course doesn't mean that we cannot enjoy what we do. But only that we should never forget the serious side of our work.

We must too, in the pursuit of our work, approach our subject matter to a certain degree with a somewhat skeptical eye. We must prove first what it is not, before we can prove what it may be. When we remove the element of doubt, as much as possible, then we can begin to make our case as to what it is and what has occurred. This approach is, of course, one of the basic foundations of scientific investigation.

Also, it must be said here, that to investigate things of a spiritual nature one must approach the subject with a somewhat religious or spiritual basis. You don't go to a Chinese restaurant and order Italian food, just as you don't try to play baseball with a hockey stick. So these things of a spiritual matter must be handled in the correct way. In certain instances of malevolent and dangerous manifestations our clients should definitely have the option available of a religious answer or the help of clergy. Also it should be noted that to truly defeat evil we must know how it works.

On the other hand, however, during the course of an investigation we cannot condone the use of psychics and psychic abilities. This does not mean that we do not believe in the psychic or sensitive tendencies that are inherent, to a certain extent, in all humans. But this intuition is built sometimes upon a certain amount of conjecture, supposition, and personal opinion. Such impressions and feelings as we all know can many times be deceiving and misleading. Therefore they cannot be considered in an investigation as a legitimate way to offer proof of scientific evidence. If investigators allow such circumstantial evidence as this, then the case itself can easily be regarded as inconclusive. This type of research cannot be considered as anywhere near a scientific approach. Without the investigative rules of science the case itself may end in failure and defeat.

As researchers of the paranormal and the supernatural our investigations should encompass all aspects of the paranormal field, not just the investigations of supposedly haunted places. But also crypto zoology, natural mysteries, unnatural light phenomenon, including UFO reports - also myths and legends of an anthropological nature that pertain to certain cultures and their locations. In short, anything considered above the normal, of course, is what we call Paranormal. In a true investigation these things and others should by all means be looked into by us with, as always, a scientific approach to the subject at hand. Unless we begin to hold ourselves to a higher calling, we as investigators and our research will never be taken seriously by those of the scientific community and by the public at large. We must always be on guard, for to lose our credibility would be to forfeit a really valuable tool that researchers of any kind could not possibly do without.

There is in the end, nothing wrong and everything right in the ever ongoing quest for knowledge. However, we must hold ourselves true to the best way in which to acquire that knowledge. We must remember too, that there will always be those that do not understand and are fearful and those that will laugh and scoff at what we do. These are all normal human reactions to the deep seeded fear of the unknown that is present in all higher forms of life. We can tolerate the tag of "ghost hunter" even though it tends to stereotype us in our true calling, but this too is all part of the job that we have set before us. So let us therefore not be afraid as we face the unknown in our quest, nor let the fear of ridicule stop us. For in the end we have made the choice - to go where few others before have gone -to bravely face what is unknown - and make it known - to see - the unseen.

Chapter 1

The Beginning

"I have always been fascinated by the mysteries of this world…that is why I investigate the unknown and the unexplained. We must never cease to push forward the boundaries of science and knowledge in our search for the truth. For the integrity of that quest alone, in the end, may truly define us as the beings that we really are…"

Dennis W. Carroll

Brandon's Story

Every person that pursues the paranormal has a reason as to why they began. Some people only have simple curiosity as their driving force. Others have actually experienced some sort of paranormal phenomena first hand. I, for one, have actually had a paranormal experience that has driven me. I have encountered several paranormal events throughout my life and have always dismissed them, but there is one event that took place when I was in my late teens that has stuck with me and is forever etched into my mind. I have always tried to dismiss most of the paranormal events, prior to this one event, as a trick of the eye or paranoia of being alone in the dark. However, on that cold, wet winter day in 1996 I could not dismiss the event that transpired in front of me, no matter how hard I tried. As I had alluded to before, the memory of this day and of that event is just as vivid in my mind as the day it happened. I can truly say that this was the point in my life when the paranormal had grabbed a hold of me, and it has never let go.

My parents and I lived in a rural area that had a large wooded area behind our house. We did not own the wooded area, but had been in my father's family for many years. As a matter of fact, my great-grandparents were our neighbors until they passed away when I was younger. My grandparents were, and are to this day, our neighbors on the other side. When my great-grandparents passed away the property was split between their children. The wooded area became a part of my grandparent's property for a few acres in, but the rest of the wood belonged to my great-aunt and another gentleman that I had never met. There was a creek that ran through the property and continued for several miles and I presume that it dumped into a lake that was nearby. I had actually never seen the end of creek.

During this particular winter it seemed to rain heavily almost every day. This caused the creek to swell and the beavers were keeping busy building and repairing dams. They had built dams all along the creek. It seemed that for every one I tore down they would build two. I finally stopped tearing them down. They really weren't hurting anything because the creek bed was not even close to full, plus I had a black labrador retriever and he loved to play in the water and these dams created a nice pond for him to dive in and swim around. The crazy dog even loved to swim when the water was near freezing.

There was one fine rainy day I decided to gear up in the best waterproof clothes I had and take my dog, Jake, to go swimming near a beaver dam. Of course it was raining and he knew where we were going as soon as I got him out of the kennel. Jake was always very good about staying near me when we went to the woods. I think that he wanted to make sure that I was okay because he was a very protective dog. I had never heard him growl at anyone, but I knew that he would protect me from anything.

We always started towards the woods by walking near the creek. We walked with the creek to our right and there was a hill to our left. The first part of the creek was in a ravine for a few hundred feet. As always, Jake would wander around smelling everything and marking things that he deemed was his. We had not gone too far when I saw someone at the top of the hill on my left. Now, I was not unaccustomed to seeing people passing through our property. We all used this part of the property to get from one place to another with relative ease.

I called for Jake to come because I didn't want him to jump on someone. I knew he would be muddy from playing in the rain and he loved everyone. Luckily he came to my side paying no attention to the person at the top of the hill. Of course, I was really paying no attention either. I was just going to exchange greetings as they got closer to me.

As the person drew closer I noticed that it was a younger woman that I did not recognize. She had long straight blonde hair and was wearing a white dress. I thought to myself, "What the heck is she doing in the pouring rain with a white dress on?" That is when I noticed that she did not have legs from the knee down.

I began rubbing my eyes thinking it was just an illusion and there is no way that I could be seeing this. When I removed my hand from my eyes she was still there and yes, she was still legless. I still could not believe that what I was seeing was real. I continued to think that she was all in my head and I was just hallucinating. That remained the case until Jake finally looked up.

Again, Jake was a friendly dog and loved everyone but rest assured he was going to protect me. The only reason I was holding him was because I did not want him jumping on this person and get them muddy, especially when they were crazy enough to wear a white dress in the rain. When he looked up, he apparently saw what I was looking at. He turned rigid, his tail was straight out, and his hackles were up. He looked like he was pointing at her. Another thing that struck me as odd was the fact that he was actually growling. I had never, until that day, heard him growl. So rest assured, he had certainly never growled at a person, but I was beginning to think that this was no person.

When I noticed that Jake had seen her as well, I watched her as she glided down the hill. I say glided because, as I had said, she had no legs. Jake was steadily growling, but he did not try to go after her. I believe that I was only frozen by the aspect of actually seeing a full body, aside from the missing legs of course, apparition. At the time I did not know the term full body apparition, but I knew what I was seeing was special. She was, by now, only a few yards in front of me.

She was headed towards a thicket that was overgrown near the creek. When she got close to the thicket a thought crossed my mind. I thought, "What if I let Jake go and he chases her?" So, I naturally let him go and as I predicted he ran straight for her. She never sped up nor changed course. She only continued to glide along in the same direction toward the thicket.

By the time Jake had gotten to her she had disappeared into the thicket. When I say disappeared I mean vanished completely with no trace. When Jake got to the thicket he started sniffing the area where she had vanished. I could only stand back and watch because I was still in shock over what I had just witnessed. I then noticed that Jake was making what seemed to me like a gurgling sound. This made me nervous and I tried to call to him but he paid me no attention what so ever. To ignore me was completely out of character for him. Even if he did not abide by my command, he always acknowledged me.

I finally worked up enough courage to walk over to him. I say it was courage, but I think I just wanted to be sure that Jake was okay. When I got close I called for him again and yet again he ignored me. This time I decided to run to him, grab his collar, and physically pull him away from that area. When I pulled him toward me I noticed that he was foaming at the mouth, his eyes seemed to be glazed over, and he was continuing to make that awful gurgling sound. I was then truly panicked to see my dog this way. I had no idea what was wrong with him or what to do. So, I decided to just shake his collar one good time and called his name loudly. When I did this he seemed to instantly snap back to reality. He stopped the gurgling sound, licked his lips, and started to move toward the woods sniffing like nothing ever happened.

I quickly decided that we were not going into the woods on this day. I called to him and we went back home. I could not go into the woods knowing what I just saw was real. I took Jake back, I put his leash on, and we went walking the other way. I repeatedly apologized to him for missing his swim, but I was not going back that way for a while.

Many months later I decided to tell my parents what I had seen that day. It had been weighing on my thoughts and I was hoping that telling them would relieve some of the pressure and anxiety that I was feeling. I began to tell them the story over dinner and before I got to the explanation of the woman my dad looked at me and says, "Oh, you mean that blonde headed woman with the white dress on?" I immediately dropped my fork and just stared at him. "Yeah, that's maw maw," he said flippantly while continuing to eat. My mother and I looked at each other and then back at him. I could not get over the nonchalant attitude that he took with it.

Maw maw was my great-grandmother on my father's side of the family. As you may remember, this is the one that lived next door to me when I was younger. My dad then began to tell me that he had seen her a lot after she had passed away. He said that he would mostly see her in the area that Jake and I saw her. This news really troubled my mom, but to this day she has never seen the blonde headed woman in the white dress. Still today, I think that she is happy and content about never seeing her.

I had never again seen the full body apparition like I did that day. I did, however, she her quickly out of the corner of my eye from time to time. The last time I saw her I just finished taking a shower and when I pulled the shower curtain back she was standing there. It startled me and I was not afraid or anxious this time when I saw her, but when I jumped and blinked she was gone. I told her right then to stop doing that to me and I have never seen her again. At times I wish that I never said that. I am afraid that I hurt her feelings and now that I am a paranormal investigator she does not want to come out and play.

From time to time, when I visit my parents, I will look out into the woods and wonder if I will ever see this apparition again. As this weighed on me, I decided that I was going to buy small pieces of paranormal investigation equipment and perform an investigation of my parents home. I finally got enough equipment and did this. The result was phenomenal to say the least. I believe that I captured the voice of the woman in white. You can visit my website and listen to it yourself and maybe, just maybe, you will begin to understand why I am what I am today.

Dennis' Story

Hello, my name is Dennis Carroll and I am a paranormal researcher and investigator, as well as a demonology consultant. I have investigated and consulted on hundreds of cases throughout the nation as well as internationally.

All my life, even as a very small child, I was always fascinated with the subject of the Supernatural. There was something in me, even then, that I can only describe as a hunger and thirst for knowledge of anything in the field of the paranormal, an interest even forty plus years later that is still very fresh. Here are the two incidents that started me on the road that I still travel.

When I was around the age of twelve years old, some boys that I hung around with and I decided, shall we say, to "investigate," a very old, creepy, deserted house in the neighborhood. This house had been empty for years and remained so even many years later. After we gained entrance to the inside and were looking around, I separated for a few minutes from the group. The whole place looked just like what you would see in a movie about a haunted house. There were white sheets covering all the furniture that was still in the place with a thick layer of dust and spider webs everywhere. Soon, I found myself confronted by a small and very rickety set of slanting stairs leading up to the loft of the old house. As I put my hand on the railing post to start up the steps, very suddenly a voice directly in my ear, as if someone were standing very close by my side, said, "Get Out!" I turned quickly looking all around me thinking that one of the boys was trying to play a trick on me, but I was all alone. The rest of the group was a couple of rooms away. Then and there, on that hot day in July, in a closed up house, I suddenly felt a strange wave of coldness wash over me. Just then, something spooked the boys and they went tearing out of the house. Of course, I found no reason to stay myself, so I followed close behind them. On that day, and for a long time after, I tried to convince myself and dismiss that incident as maybe a trick of sound or the atmosphere. To this day, I have never come to a satisfying conclusion in my mind as to what really happened in that experience other than it had to be something of a paranormal nature.

A few years after this had taken place, something happened that would change my outlook even more on the subject of the Supernatural, something that could have only one explanation for me. I was about sixteen years old at the time and it was during a church service that I was attending. They prayed for and initiated something of an exorcism upon a man.

The minister told everyone to bow their heads and pray and not to look up, but during the prayer, I did. As I raised my head and looked toward the front of the church, I very distinctly, without any doubt whatsoever, saw three demonic spirits leave this man one by one and disappear through a nearby wall. I can only describe them as bowling ball sized dirty spheres of dark light and the property of their actions were like nothing of the natural world that I had ever seen before.

This was no trick of the light or hallucination of any kind on my part. They were actual things but outside the realm of anything I had ever witnessed or ever thought possible. I was shocked, to say the least, and very astonished for awhile. My mind did not seem to want to believe what I had seen but eventually it began to sink in and I quickly moved beyond wonder and awe to the curiosity and fascination that still feeds my quest for knowledge to find the answers of what I seek to this day. I had found that another part of this world really does exist, the unseen part and it will always be there waiting for me. No other incident, before or since, and I have had quite a few, has fueled my interest in the Supernatural or paranormal like this did. My quest still goes on and will so until the time that I myself become a part of the vast unknown. One thing gives me comfort, however, and that is the knowledge that where there are demons there must also be angels. These incidences and much more are the reasons why I and others like me must seek the answers that are waiting…Beyond the Shadows!

"To ensure that integrity is never compromised, I will never seek for anything less than the knowledge of the truth!"

Brandon Hudgens

Veritas…Scientia…Integritas

Chapter 2

Paranormal Investigation

"Know all things to be like this: As a magician makes illusions of horses, oxen carts and other things, nothing is as it appears."

The Buddah

Our Perspective

My name is Brandon Hudgens. I am the Founder and Director of the Carolina Society for Paranormal Research and Investigation Inc (CSPRI Inc). CSPRI Inc was established on February 29, 2012. Our group may seem young, but our founding members carried over fifty years of experience between us. The original members of the group came together when we realized that our community needed a true investigation and research organization with an education and outreach frame of mind. We are comprised of a very eclectic group of individuals that have come together with one vision and one mission. We are comprised of members with experience in the field of investigation, history, case management, photography, research, the supernatural, folklore, marketing, carpentry, engineering, the occult, and much more.

The CSPRI Inc mission is a simple one, we want to investigate, educate and outreach. We feel that by openly sharing information and evidence with the paranormal community we can further the communal cause. We have no reason to hide anything that we discover because we are all working toward the same goal. It astounds me to see certain groups that hoard their findings and discoveries and keep everything to themselves. It is my thought that these groups are only out for popularity or notoriety. In my humble opinion, the more you share and help other groups, the greater your name will become by default. Your group will then become synonymous with integrity, and with integrity comes respect. Respect is the main concept that CSPRI Inc is working toward.

This book is an attempt at educating those that want to pursue becoming the best paranormal investigator that they can possibly be. Paranormal investigation is a scientific endeavor that needs as much help as it can get. This field is a labor of love because there is little to no money to be made. If you are able to make a living doing what you love, my hat is off to you. However, what this field truly needs are individuals that understand the importance of advancing the field of the paranormal. Treating paranormal investigation as pure entertainment will not only hurt the investigator but the client as well. It is sad to say that the best and worst thing to happen to this field was the introduction of paranormal investigation to the world via main-stream television.

I don't want you to think that I am pontificating on the morals of paranormal investigation. However, I do want you to understand where we are coming from and where we stand on the core value of paranormal investigation. That core value is advancing the paranormal field. I hope that what you have read is not going to turn you away from this book, but hopefully has caught your interest in what we are going to say over the next nine chapters. As I have mentioned, we are here to educate and share our knowledge with you.

You do not have to agree with everything we have to say and we welcome your feedback. We feel that feedback, positive or negative, is what helps this field grow.

Thank you very much for your interest in this book. I hope that you enjoy it as much as we loved writing it!

Ghost Hunting, Paranormal Investigating It's All The Same. Isn't it?

I have been asked by a lot of people about ghost hunting and paranormal investigation. Well, you may be asking yourself right now, "Why do they sometimes call it ghost hunting and sometimes paranormal investigation? Isn't it the same thing?" Amazingly enough there is a huge difference. I consider myself a paranormal investigator not just a ghost hunter. Yes at times I am a ghost hunter, but more often than not I am not simply hunting ghosts. In this section we will finally give you the answer to this debated question.

Before I begin on this subject I want to tell you why I am devoting an entire section to it. There are many individuals and groups in this field that get quite upset if you call them Ghost Hunters. I can only speak for myself on this subject. I do prefer to be called a paranormal investigator over being called a ghost hunter. I am not trying to be haughty about titles by any means. It is simply a matter of distinction and function.

Ghost hunting, for the most part, is exactly what it says. It is act of seeking paranormal events for sport and excitement. These individuals go in search of a high, to just have fun, or to simply be social. One example of ghost hunters is the formation of social groups that generally meet in graveyards, cemeteries, abandoned schools, old churches, and so on. These individuals get together for nothing more than socializing and to be seen. They have no interest in the advancement of the paranormal field nor do they wish to help anyone that is frightened, concerned, or needs questions answered. At times these individuals can cause the activity to increase and possibly become more violent. These individuals on occasion have issues with entities attaching themselves to them. I have actually had many cases where we were called in because this has happened.

Don't think that I dislike ghost hunters. On the contrary, I think that this is a valid hobby. I have partaken in ghost hunting on occasion. It is a great way to get together with friends, have a good time, and possibly get some training in. However, you must always make sure that you are having a good time legally. All too often these individuals break the law in the name of ghost hunting. For instance, it is illegal to be in cemeteries and graveyards after sundown and before sunup without express permission from the owners. Trespassing is the other side of ghost hunting that gives the true paranormal investigator a bad name. It also puts up barriers that make it so much more difficult for paranormal investigators to get permission to investigate historic locations. I run into this barrier much too often.

Paranormal investigation, on the other hand, is going to a location that has known activity and gathering data to prove or debunk the activity. This activity may not only be related to ghost sightings. It can be related to UFOs, cryptozoological studies, demonic or angelic sightings, etc. The paranormal investigator also has an obligation to help the owner of the location that they are investigating. The help includes educating the owner of the activity, giving options on how to handle the situation, or directing them to other groups that are better suited to help. Offering options for help is what makes the paranormal investigator stand out.

Paranormal investigators also take pride in themselves in their professionalism. To consider yourself a paranormal investigator you must present yourself like you would in any business situation. I do not want to give you the idea that we are a stick in the mud, however, we do what we do because we want to help people. Looking the part is only the beginning of professionalism. Meeting the clients for the first time to investigate a private residence generally sends the wrong impression when you show up in shorts and flip-flops. I am not saying that you need to show up in a three piece suit to interview clients, but show pride in yourself and your group. I generally wear a nice pair of jeans or slacks and a polo shirt. It would even be great if you could get a polo shirt with your teams logo embroidered on it. That appearance generally conveys professionalism to the client and makes them feel more at ease.

Paranormal investigators also use various tools to help gather data. They include video recorders, audio recorders, temperature recording devices, magnetic field detectors, and many more tools. Later in the book I will go over these tools and more and I will also somewhat explain how they are used. A ghost hunter generally has a camera and an audio recorder. These are great tools, but so much more data is required to gain a full understanding of the claims that were made.

Another type of paranormal investigator is the paranormal researcher. The paranormal researcher is one of the most important functions of being a paranormal investigator. If you are deeming yourself a paranormal investigator you must learn one basic lesson: YOU MUST PERFORM RESEARCH! If you are part of a group that has researchers on staff then you are already a step ahead of the game and are offering the clients the best possible service.

Research can be on any topic. For instance, you are reading this book and that in itself is considered research. You may read the same type of material over and over, but there is that one time you may see something in a different light or written a slightly different way and instantly you have a better understanding. This happens to me a lot and to be truthful, I still learn something new about this field at least once a week. You may also read several publications and are in some way able to connect the material together. This is what drives a lot of researchers to continue to read and dig into various materials. This type of research also advances our field when we are able to use it and connect the dots.

Research is not limited to only the paranormal. Paranormal investigators/researchers may run into a variety of things that they must have at least some knowledge of. They need to be aware of anthropology, biology, psychology, history, construction, astronomy, and much more. These things can never be mastered together. If anyone ever tells you that they are an expert paranormal investigator, they are lying to you. There are no true experts in this field, although having a professional attitude is always a must.

I hope now that you have a better understanding of the terms ghost hunter and paranormal investigator. Like I have said, there is nothing wrong with being a ghost hunter. It just simply has its place and time. My hopes are that as you continue to read this book you will realize that being a paranormal investigator is so much more rewarding. If you are content on being a ghost hunter, well you may as well close this book, smile, and patiently wait until your next hunt.

"That what is yielding and tender belongs to the realm of life, and what is hard and strong belongs to the realm of death."

Lao Tse

Chapter 3

Science and Religion

"Science without religion is lame. Religion without science is blind."

Albert Einstein

The Scientific Method

I am sure that most people reading this have had some sort of science class in school and have some sense of what the Scientific Method is. I define the Scientific Method as a method of research in which a problem is identified, relevant data is gathered, a hypothesis is formulated from this data, and the hypothesis is empirically tested. You can then either accept the hypothesis or reject the hypothesis. Rejecting the hypothesis does not mean that the experiment was a failure. This only means that you must formulate another hypothesis.

Let us go a step further and go into a little more detail. The exact number of steps to the Scientific Method depends on how you divide the steps. If you take a look at Figure 1 you will see how we break up the steps.

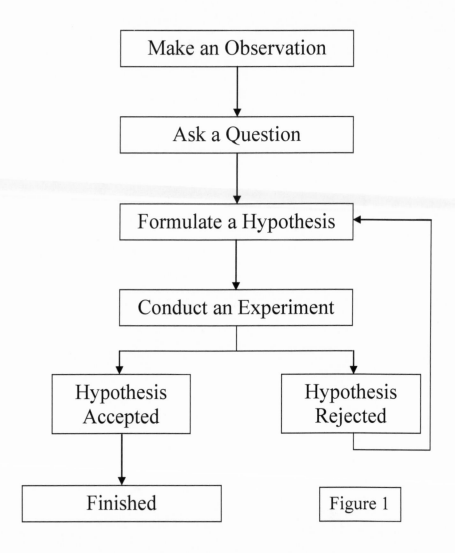

Figure 1

I would like to now give you a deeper explanation of these steps so that you will, hopefully, gain a deeper understanding.

Scientific Method Step 1: Make an Observation.

Many people make the mistake of thinking that the Scientific Method begins by forming a hypothesis. The main reason behind this mistake is because most observations are made informally. After all, when you are looking for a project idea you think through all of the things you have experienced (observations you have made) and try to find one that would be suitable for an experiment. The informal variation of Step 1 does work, however, you will have a richer source of ideas if you pick a subject and write down observations until suitable test idea is available. Let us say that you want to do an experiment but you need an idea. Take what is around you and start writing down observations. WRITE DOWN EVERYTHING! This includes colors, timing, sounds, temperatures, light levels, etc.

Scientific Method Step 2: Ask a Question.

When observations are made the next natural step is to simply ask a question. This question could encompass anything that you have observed that you do not fully understand. The most basic questions to ask are: Who? What? When? Where? Why? How? You do need to ensure that your question can be quantified by some measure and that it is not ambiguous. It is very important to remember that you are going to run a series of tests to answer this question.

Scientific Method Step 3: Formulate a Hypothesis.

A hypothesis is a statement that can be used to predict the outcome of future observations. The null hypothesis, or no-difference hypothesis, is a good type of hypothesis to test. An example of a null hypothesis is stating that the rate at which grass grows is not dependent on the amount of light it receives. You see, even if you feel that light affects how the grass grows, it is easier to disprove that light has no effect than to get into a more complex detail of how much light grass needs or at what wavelength grass grows best. Further experiments can be derived from this one hypothesis, but you need to concentrate on accepting or rejecting one at a time. In other words, do not test the effects of light and water at the same time until they have been tested separately. Remember that it is very important to only test one hypothesis at a time and to state the hypothesis in a way that it will be easily tested.

Scientific Method Step 4: Design and Conduct an Experiment

There are many different ways to test a single hypothesis. If I wanted to test the null hypothesis, the rate of grass growth is not dependent on quantity of light. I would first have grass exposed to no light and this is called the control group. A control group is identical in every

52

way to the other experimental groups except for the variable being tested. I would also have grass with light called the experimental group. I could complicate the experiment by having differing levels of light, different types of grasses, etc. Let me stress that the control group can only differ from any experimental groups with respect to the one variable. For example, in all fairness I could not compare grass in my yard in the shade and grass in the sun... there are other variables between the two groups besides light, such as moisture and probably pH of the soil (where I am it is more acidic near the trees and buildings, which is also where it is shady). Keep your experiment as simple as possible.

Now it is time to perform the experiment. Your data might take the form of numbers, yes/no, present/absent, or other observations. It is important to keep data that "looks bad." Many experiments have been sabotaged by researchers throwing out data that did not agree with preconceptions. KEEP ALL OF THE DATA! You can make notes if something exceptional occurred when a particular data point was taken. Also, it is a good idea to write down observations related to your experiment that aren't directly related to the hypothesis. These observations could include variables over which you have no control, such as humidity, temperature, vibrations, or any noteworthy happenings.

Scientific Method Step 5: Accept or Reject the Hypothesis

For some experiments, conclusions may be formed based on an informal analysis of the data. This can be accomplished by simply asking, "Does the data fit the hypothesis." This is one way to consider accepting or rejecting a hypothesis. However, it is best to apply a statistical analysis to data. You should do this in order to establish a degree of acceptance or rejection. Mathematics is most useful in assessing the effects of measurement errors and other uncertainties in an experiment. It is important to remember when using statistics you should always look for outlying data. These points are sometimes anomalous events and should not be included in the data unless the outlier is pertinent to the outcome.

Hypothesis Accepted? Things to Remember

Accepting a hypothesis does not guarantee that it was the correct hypothesis. This only means that the results of your experiment support the hypothesis that you rendered. Keep in mind that it is still possible to duplicate the experiment and get a different result the next time. It is also possible to have a hypothesis that explains the observations, yet is not the explanation that is desired. Remember, a hypothesis can be disproven but never proven.

Hypothesis Rejected? Back to Step 2

If the null hypothesis was rejected, that may be as far as your experiment needs to go. That is just saying that the null hypothesis did not matter and usually that is what you are attempting to prove. If any other hypothesis was rejected, then it is time to reconsider your explanation for your observations. At least you won't be starting from scratch. You will now have more observations and data than ever before. You may also want to consider the experiment and wish to change it slightly.

At this point it would simply be best to go over real example of how this method can be used during a paranormal investigation. It is always important to remain unbiased and always ask the correct questions. It is also extremely important to keep in mind that during all stages of the scientific process of investigation to note that all information gathered during the process should be checked and re-checked for authenticity and integrity. The knowledge accumulated using this method is essential to the final outcome of your investigation.

Let's say that you are performing an investigation outside away from any power lines or AC power sources. You then notice that your K-II meter is starting to blink while your partner is checking in with command central. Instead of moving straight to paranormal phenomena, you ask yourself, "Do the two-way radios interfere with my K-II meter?"

You then need to form a hypothesis. In this case the hypothesis would be, "I believe that my K-II is triggered by frequencies emitted by the two-way radio." The hypothesis needs to be a definitive statement. This particular hypothesis is based upon two thoughts: K-II meters measure electro-magnetic fields and by observation, the K-II seemed to be affected by the two-way radio when it was used. Using this hypothesis, you predict that the K-II meter will activate when the two-way radio is in use.

To set up this experiment you will need several different types of two-way radios and several K-II meters. Use the two-way radios and document the affect on the K-II meter. After all of the documentation is collected it must be analyzed. However, if you are in the field you must use the equipment you have available. Try several different scenarios with the two-way radio and document your findings.

After the data has been analyzed you will find if the results have supported or rejected your hypothesis. If the hypothesis has been rejected then you start over by formulating another hypothesis and repeat the previous steps. Remember that an experiment isn't a failure if it proves your hypothesis wrong or if it proves your prediction isn't accurate. An experiment is only a failure if there is a flaw in the design.

I support the use of the Scientific Method over all other forms of paranormal investigation. My group employs the use of the Scientific Method in all of their paranormal research and investigations. I do understand the paranormal is a very spiritual classification. However, we should strive to find evidence in a non-objective way.

Metaphysics

There are many different types of paranormal investigation methods to choose from. Though, in this book there are two methods that we are really attempting to concentrate on. I want to discuss the Metaphysical approach to paranormal investigation as well as the Scientific Method approach to paranormal investigation.

Let us first consider Metaphysics. Metaphysics is defined as the branch of philosophy that uses the idea of origin principles or explaining the nature of being and existence. These principles include ontology, cosmology, and are intimately connected to epistemology. I know that this is a lot of –ology to throw at you, but keep in mind that Metaphysics has been developing since the ancient times of Aristotle. Most people give Aristotle credit for beginning the thought process of Metaphysics, but Aristotle himself credits earlier philosophers for this.

Now I want to break Metaphysics down even further, so we can define each of the branches. Let's begin with Ontology. Ontology is defined as the nature of being. This branch of philosophy deep dives into the nature of human and spiritual existence and the perception of reality. Ontology serves to question and to quantify existence and reality. The main question is simply, what is the meaning of being? This basic question is what seems to drive the paranormal side of the

Metaphysics philosophy. Once the paranormal investigator has begun to question being, they may then dive further into the philosophy. This then poses two inherent questions of paranormal investigation. What is existence? What is the property of existence? These are the beginning points to ponder when performing a deep dive into a Metaphysical investigation.

Cosmology is the next philosophical idea in Metaphysics. This is defined as understanding the origin of the universe and how the universe is structured. Cosmology also looks at the laws of the universe and trying to understand how the universe remains in order and not in a constant state of chaos. Today, Paranormal Metaphysicians have morphed this idea into a new idea called Esoteric Cosmology or Esotericism. Esotericism now begins to dive into planes of existence, hierarchies of spirits, altered states of conscientiousness, and mysticism. There is much more to Esotericism, but these are the main themes that deal with the paranormal and the investigation of the paranormal. The New Age movement has seemed to concentrate on this area of metaphysics for their investigative procedures. This movement uses altered states of conscientiousness and mysticism to "call" the spirits to them. This is when they begin to investigate their interactions. I consider this dangerous because you never know what you are opening yourself up to. We feel that is very important that under no circumstance should you alter your consciousness or your mind in any form or fashion. This includes alcohol, drugs, meditation, etc. There are too many dangers in the paranormal and I NEVER RECOMMEND DOING THIS!

The last branch of Metaphysics is Epistemology. This is the understanding of the nature, methods, and limits of human knowledge. Epistemology is also connected to belief, skepticism, and our understanding of truth. These three factors are what paranormal investigators bring to the forefront during investigations. Even if you do not subscribe to Metaphysics as a basis for paranormal investigation, it is good to have an understanding of Epistemology because of the connection of this branch to skepticism and belief. Belief is simply thinking or believing something is true even without having proof of it being true. For instance, I believe that this house is haunted. I have never seen, spoke to, nor touched the spirits in the house, but in my mind they exist. Faith, or trust, is the largest proponent for this cognitive response. Skepticism is the direct opposite of belief. A skeptic will not accept a belief as truth until it has been proven to them. With the previous example the skeptic would say that the house is not haunted because they have not seen, spoke to, nor touched the spirits. Truth, in this case, is something that is actually known and cannot be proven as anything else. An example of this is the truth that water is wet. This is a truth and there is no one in the world that can refute this. Truth is the amazing intersection where belief becomes knowledge and skepticism becomes enlightenment.

Epistemology is the precursor to modern day paranormal investigation. Our forefathers of the paranormal field either had a belief of the paranormal or were very skeptical of the belief that there were spirits among us. This is why they began to search for the truth.

I know that this may be all very confusing. That is why Metaphysics is considered to be a philosophy and not a science. However, if you decide to travel the path of Metaphysics, you must understand all of the points of this philosophy. True Metaphysical investigators use all of the branches and not just certain parts of it. Sadly, Metaphysics has steered away from philosophical pondering to what is considered to be the New Age Enlightenment. These practitioners of the New Age Enlightenment are now beginning to bring in past occult practices to the field of paranormal investigation and calling it Metaphysical and/or Esoterical. These individuals are among those that strictly following the Esoteric Cosmology branch. Most of these Metaphysical investigations include, but are not limited to, dowsing, the use of psychics/mediums, the use of Ouija boards, séances, remote viewing, etc.

I am not trying to say that these methods do not exist or are not real. All of these techniques are very real and they will produce results. However, the caveat is, they can be very dangerous to the investigation personnel and most importantly to the client. The problem lies in the method of most paranormal investigators that use these methods. For instance, instead of asking the spirits if they are there, you are calling them to you. This could lead to a nasty run in with violent spirits or demonic entities. This generally results in the client having a harder time after the investigation is finished. It also makes it harder for the client to rid themselves of these entities. There are a select few that have enough knowledge of Metaphysics to protect themselves and the client, but it takes years to master and the journey is very dangerous. This is the overall reason as to why I do not suggest this method.

One of the greatest flaws in this method, that I have found, is the simple fact that it plants a seed of actual activity in everyone's mind. This means if I was to go in and perform a séance at a location and tell everyone that there is a ghost of a little boy there, I am sure that every investigator will be looking for the spirit of a little boy. In some instances I am sure that they will find this spirit. This is called subjectification. I know that some groups use psychics, séances, etc. after their investigation, but it still plants the seed for those that are reviewing the evidence. If you really want to use this method please ensure that your paranormal investigation and your Metaphysical investigation remains absolutely separate.

Now I hope you see my reservations with the Metaphysical approach to paranormal investigation. I am merely giving my opinion on this type of method because, well, this is my book. However, if this is the path that you choose to follow, then please do not let me talk you out of it. All I ask is that you collectively research ALL methods and take extreme care when doing so. This not only affects you and your team, but it affects your client as well.

Religion

There is a massive debate on whether or not paranormal investigation or ghost hunting goes against the basic principles of the Christian faith. To be honest, I even struggled with this concept before stepping into the paranormal field. I had to do a lot of research and ask many people a lot of questions. I know that there are some investigators out there that are not Christian and you may feel that this section has no bearing on you at all. Our intention is not to leave those of you that do not practice Christianity out, but to simply put it, the organization that I am a part of is Christian and I must address this from our organizations point of view. So, if you feel that this section is not for you, please feel free to jump this section of the book. However, I truly hope that you do not skip ahead. As it is in all aspects of the paranormal, learning things about another religion can also be helpful to you at some point down the road. Who knows, there may come a day that a client needs help understanding the paranormal in this point of view and you will be able to help them.

If you have decided to keep reading, I am extremely grateful that you have opened your mind to this section. First, let me explain Christianity to those of you who just may not know. We are sure that you have heard of it at least, simply because one third of the world's population follows this religion. Christianity follows the belief that

Jesus is the Messiah that was prophesied in the Old Testament of the Bible. There are also many denominations of Christianity, such as: Catholic, Protestant, Methodist, Baptist, Lutheran, etc. Though these denominations vary in how God is worshipped, each denomination has one major element in common; they all believe that Jesus is the lord and savior of every man, woman and child. They also believe that the only way to enter heaven is by confessing your sins and accepting Jesus as your lord and savior. This is where the similarities of the religions fall away. They all have their small nuances that make them different.

Now with that said and out of the way we can get back to how Christianity intertwines with paranormal investigation. Some denominations feel that consorting with spirits is against God's will. The largest majority of the people arguing this point derive their argument from Deuteronomy 18: 9-18 (KJV). The scripture I am referring to is as follows:

9. When thou art come into the land which the LORD thy God giveth thee, thou shalt not learn to do after the abominations of those nations.

10. There shall not be found among you any one that maketh his son or his daughter to pass

through the fire, or that useth divination, or an observer of times, or an enchanter, or a witch.

11. Or a charmer, or a consulter with familiar spirits, or a wizard, or a necromancer.

12. For all that do these things are an abomination unto the LORD: and because of these abominations the LORD thy God doth drive them out from before thee.

My first argument for this is simply that this scripture is in the Old Testament or better known as the Torah. The Torah, for all intents and purposes, is the instruction manual for the Israelites. I am not saying that we should not read this and use it, but we are not bound by God to follow the numerous laws of the Old Testament. The only laws that we, non-Jewish people or Gentiles, are bound to can be found in Galatians 2: 16-21 (KJV). That is much different that the numerous laws that the Jews must adhere to. Galatians 2: 16-21 (KJV) reads as follows:

16. Knowing that a man is not justified by the works of the law, but by the faith of Jesus Christ, even we have believed in Jesus Christ, that we might be justified by the faith of

Christ, and not by the works of the law: for by the works of the law shall no flesh be justified.

17. But if, while we seek to be justified by Christ, we ourselves also are found sinners, is therefore Christ the minister of sin? God forbid.

18. For if I build again the things which I destroyed, I make myself a transgressor.

19. For I through the law am dead to the law, that I might live unto God.

20. I am crucified with Christ: nevertheless I live; yet not I, but Christ liveth in me: and the life which I now live in the flesh I live by the faith of the Son of God, who loved me, and gave himself for me.

21. I do not frustrate the grace of God: for if righteousness come by the law, then Christ is dead in vain.

Now that we got the theological part of the argument over, we can get to the true argument. We as paranormal investigators are not actually consulting with spirits. We are also not seeking information about our futures or our fate. We are simply asking if there is a spirit there and asking what they want. There is a scripture in the New Testament that actually tells us that what we are doing is not only right, but is encouraged. In 1 John 4:1-2 (KJV) we are tasked with testing the spirit to see if it is of God. The scripture is as follows:

1. Dear friends, do not believe every spirit, but test the spirits to see whether they are from God, because many false prophets have gone out into the world.

2. This is how you can recognize the Spirit of God: Every spirit that acknowledges that Jesus Christ has come in the flesh is from God.

So, now we can see that we do have confirmation that what we do is perfectly fine within the confines of the scriptural concepts. We are not going against God and committing a sin. We are simply attempting to find out what is there and find out what it wants or why it is there.

You can see that this is a short section and that is the way that I intended it to be. To me this concept is simple and really does not require a lot of writing. If you so chose, there are many blogs and articles on the internet that argue for and against this concept. I simply wanted to show you my version and allow you to think for yourself. If you are not a believer, yet you read this section, Thank You.

"The most beautiful experience we can have is the mysterious. It is the fundamental emotion which stands at the cradle of all true art and science. Whoever does not know it and can no longer wonder, no longer marvel, is as good as dead, and his eyes are dimmed.

It was the experience of mystery – even mixed with fear – that engendered religion. A knowledge of the existence of something we cannot penetrate, our perceptions of the profoundest reason and the most radiant beauty, which only in their most primitive forms are accessible to our minds – it is this knowledge and this emotion that constitute true religiosity; in this sense, and in this alone, I am a deeply religious man."

Albert Einstein

Chapter 4

What Makes an Investigation?

"When you have eliminated the impossible, then whatever remains, however improbable, must be the truth."

Sherlock Holmes

The Investigation

We are finally to that point where you, the investigator, are ready to begin investigating the paranormal. Most investigators begin by blindly going into a location with their fancy new high-tech equipment and just start doing what they see on television. This is the absolute worst thing that you can do! Believe it or not, there is a step by step process you should follow before even thinking about the physical investigation. This section is designed to help you think through an investigation from beginning to end. By reading this section you are committing yourself to becoming an elite paranormal investigator. If you wish only to investigate only for a thrill, this is not the section for you. The best way to explain an investigation is simply going through a step-by-step analysis from beginning to end. Here we go!

1. Opening the Case

The first part of any investigation is to open a case file. A case file allows you to put all of your information that you gather about the case in one easy to find location. This file should be categorized so that you can easily and quickly find information. The file may be electronic, paper, or a combination but it is important to keep all of the information you gather together. For example, when our group opens a case file we give it a number such as 130102. This may look like just a long number but in reality it means something to us. The 13 signifies the year that the case was opened. Having the year first allows us quick access to a yearly subgroup. The 01 signifies the month that the case was opened. This further breaks the subgroup down to easily identify a specific case. The 02 indicates what case in that month we are working with. So, case number 130102 is the second case in January, 2013. To further illustrate when we open the first case in February, 2013 that case number will be 130201. This allows us to quickly identify certain cases and it automatically keeps them in chronological order. You are probably thinking that this information is non-sense, however, if you want to be a serious investigator you need to have a system like this in place.

2. Interview the Client

After you have decided on a system to categorize your cases, you need to begin by asking the client a series of questions to get more information from them about the case. Sometimes, within the interview you may hit on key points that may lead you in a direction to help them. This means it is very important to devise your questions to cover as much ground about the client as possible. At times it is prudent to ask very specific and intimate details about their life. It may be embarrassing but it needs to be done. You also need to ensure that you are not dealing with someone that is taking mind altering drugs, someone that has a history of mental issues, or simply someone that could pose a threat to you and your team. One important aspect of interviewing a client is to do it in person if possible. If you are interviewing a client in person, it will be easier to pick up on certain mannerisms that you would be unable to do on the phone or through email. When you are meeting the client for the first time, it is best to do it in a neutral public location. This will give the client a piece of mind when meeting the strangers that they are about to let into their lives for the first time. Meeting the client in public is also a safety precaution for you. This allows you to decide if the client is trustworthy enough to allow your team into their domain. Remember, the number one rule in any investigation is safety.

3. Perform a Walkthrough of the Location

Now that you have met the client, they have passed all of your interview questions, and you have accepted the case, the next step is to view the location. If at all possible this should NOT be done on the day of the investigation. This should be done prior to the investigation so that you can plan how to prepare for the investigation. Sketch an outline of the location and if possible take measurements for the sketch. Also, take the opportunity to take photos of the location and make sure you can identify the photographed area on the sketch. Taking photos is very important when trying to determine where to set up your equipment because it gives you an idea of the depth of each room or location. If you have static IR cameras that you would like to set up these pictures can give you an idea of how to do this without the cameras affecting each other. Performing the walkthrough also gives you an idea of how the client feels in certain areas of the location and this gives you an idea of where to spend more time during your investigation. The most important thing that you can do at the walkthrough comes at the end. You need to have the client start a journal, if they have not already, detailing any activity that happens after you leave that day. That journal needs to be very detailed with time, location, and experience. This gives you, the investigator, more to go on when you arrive for the investigation.

4. Prepare for the Investigation

After the walkthrough the case leader needs to decide what equipment would be best suited for the location and what personnel may be needed for the investigation. The sketch and photographs will provide a true visualization of where the equipment should be set up and it outlines the perimeter of the investigation area. It is best to have all of the equipment that is needed in specified cases that are marked. This will allow for quick access and a smoother set up. There is nothing more time consuming than searching for the correct equipment while setting up. It is also not very professional to search through cases for equipment while the client is watching. Once the equipment has been staged, a plan for the amount of personnel and how they will be used during the investigation is needed. It would be ideal if a schedule were written down and given to everyone before you go to the location. This is to keep anyone from getting confused on the job that they are to perform. When the schedule is given to the investigators it is extremely crucial to show them the boundaries of the investigation perimeter. This perimeter should never be breached unless an investigation is in progress. A meeting needs to be organized to ensure that all of the personnel have an understanding of how the equipment works and how it needs to be set up before the investigation day. This meeting is crucial to a smooth set up even if the team has worked together for a long time.

5. The Investigation

Now we can finally get to the fun part of doing what we do. The investigation should go very smoothly, only if you have prepared well enough. The important thing about an investigation is having everyone on the same page. Prior to arriving to the location, or as soon as the team gets to the location, a prayer of protection needs to be said. No matter what religious affiliation you may be a part of, this is important. This will help to seal the team in the event a spirit tries to attach itself to one or more of the team. Upon arriving to the location the case leader needs to greet the client and ask for the journal, if they had any further activity. While the case leader and the client discuss the journal, the team should be getting the equipment staged for setting up. Not only does this streamline the investigation, but it gives the client a piece of mind that professionals are here and they know what they are doing. The case leader then takes the tech team in and shows them where to set up the static equipment. The tech team should already have an idea of how the setup should take place from the meeting that should have taken place before the investigation. The tech team then takes over and the equipment should be set up with minimal obstructions, only if you had taken the time to prepare for the investigation. The tech team is in charge of the equipment but this does not exempt any of the other members from helping with the set up. It is called a team after all. No piece of equipment should leave the staging area without the tech team leader knowing that it is removed. The tech team leader should only let a piece of equipment out of sight after they have checked it off of their list. This not only helps keep track of what is being used, it ensures that all of the equipment is accounted for. It may be best if you have the team members provide their own basic equipment. This will ensure that the team's equipment is not damaged and if it is personal equipment it will be cared for even better. I know that it would not be prudent for every member to have static cameras, temp pods, etc. but mobile equipment is cheap enough and sturdy enough now for everyone to have their own.

Keep in mind that it would be impossible to prepare for every contingency, but you should at least be prepared for most. No one has ever failed by being over prepared for anything. After the set up is finished and the case leader is happy with the set up, it is time to let the location "cool down." This gives the location time to settle from all of the traffic and noise of the set up. The cool down period should last no less than an hour before the first team infiltrates the perimeter. Once it is time to begin investigation, only the teams investigating should breach the perimeter and everyone should be as quiet as possible. You can have more than one team in different areas, but you need to ensure that neither team will contaminate the others evidence collection. The night is then spent with teams investigating. Make sure that you put a break in during the investigation. This will also allow the location another cool down period. The investigation will not end until the case leader calls it, or the allotted time has been covered.

6. The Breakdown

At the end of the investigation it is time to gather all of the equipment, pack up, and leave the location. The best way I have found to do this is to have one person that is responsible for ensuring all of the equipment is gathered. This person should be the tech team leader since they know the equipment better than most of the team and the simple fact that this person should have been checking out the equipment as it was taken from the case. Have the tech team leader located in one position checking in the equipment as the ENTIRE TEAM breaks it all down. Our team's rule is no one is exempt from the breakdown and that includes the case leader and the director. This not only helps thing go a little faster, but it keeps the morale high and the jealousy low. Once all of the equipment is packed and the team is ready to leave, the case leader needs to speak to the client once more and explain what the next steps are and what they should expect in the coming days. After the case leader is done the team needs to meet at either the location or at a specified location close to the investigation site. This is the time that the case leader talks about the investigation and a prayer to seal the group from any unwanted tag-along needs to be said. Again, no matter what religious affiliation you have any variation of a prayer needs to be said.

7. The Evidence Review

The evidence review is the most crucial part of the entire investigation. This is when any evidence of paranormal activity is found and verified. Evidence review is very painstaking and time consuming. However, every second of each piece of equipment must be reviewed in real time. For instance, if you have an eight hour investigation and you used four static cameras that will be twenty-four hours of real time review that needs to be viewed. This does not include audio, personal video, photographs, or any other recordings that may have been made. Audio and video review should never be done simultaneously. You need to focus on one thing at a time to give the evidence a fair and unimpeded review. Evidence review consumes so much time that it is best that it be split between all of the team members and done in time slots with rest periods. This does not include the time that you need to work or spend with your family. After the initial review is done and all of the notes are made it is best to go back over the areas you have noted. Spend time on this section to ensure that it cannot be explained in some fashion. If you have the resources it is best to have the evidence reviewed twice by different people. This will ensure that nothing was overlooked. Nothing is 100% when it comes to reviewing evidence. Things are missed all of the time, but it needs to be done as thoroughly as possible. Once the evidence is collected and separated you should then turn it over to the case leader for their review. The case leader then can sort through what they perceive as good evidence or not so good evidence. The case leader then should bring the evidence to the director for the final verdict. After all, it is the responsibility of the director to keep the integrity of their group intact.

8. The Reveal

The reveal, to some, is the most exciting part of the investigation. This is most definitely the most exciting part for the client. If you have your group set up as we do, the case leader is in charge of the case from inception to close. The director only passes the final judgment. This means that the case leader performs the reveal in our group with the assistant director and director as support. With that said, the case leader meets the client at either the location or another pre-determined location to go over the case. Once the evidence is presented to the client and the questions are answered about the case, the case leader can get an idea of where the client would like to go from there. Our group offers spiritual cleansings or house blessings to those that may want that option. The client may want another investigation if their curiosity is not satisfied or, on the other hand, they may be satisfied and wish to go no further. It is always up to the client to choose what they wish to do, but you as an investigator can offer suggestions if the client seems to be torn or undecided. Whatever the case may be, the client is the one person that every team must satisfy. If the client wishes to continue, the case leader plans another investigation with the help of the case manager. If they are satisfied it is simply time to close the case. Sometimes the client may be torn between more help or simply leaving it alone. That is when we leave the case open and keep in contact with the client until they are satisfied. Like I had stated before, it is the client that must be happy.

9. Closing the Case

As in all situations the case can only be closed by the director. The case leader may lend suggestions on how to proceed with the case. Personally, I usually go along with the suggestion of the case leader, except in an extreme circumstance. If the case is closed, all of the files need to be kept together in a secure location. The files should be accessible if the need arises to reopen the case or needing research information on a different case. That is why I suggest to you to back-up and store all of your video, audio, and pictures. You never know when the need will arise that you have to break out that evidence again and have another review. It is always a good idea to keep everything that you captured as archival data. Data storage has become cheaper, so why not keep everything you can.

Investigation Protocols

Small Area

In a small area of coverage, such as a small room in a house, you will in many ways approach it as you do in larger rooms, but with a slight difference. We will discuss the larger rooms in detail later in this section. Smaller rooms are very simple and easy to navigate and generally only one investigator is needed to perform this investigation protocol.

The first thing to keep in mind is finding the center of this area from the entrance. Once you move to the center of this area you may begin to take your base readings, observations, photographs, etc. from each point of the compass (North, South, East, and West). After this return the entrance of the small area. From here you should follow the perimeter moving slowly in a clockwise or counter clockwise direction. Just remember to continue to move in that direction once you are committed. Continue your observations, readings, etc. as you move along the perimeter.

You will eventually make your way back to the entrance from where you began. This is meant to be a very thorough, quick, and complete way to cover a small area. This is by no means a replacement for investigations. Sitting and waiting is still by far the best method. We simply want to give you a means to cover these areas and log the best base readings. Please review Figure 1 for a visual of this protocol.

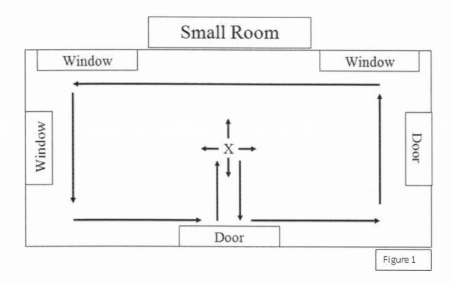

Figure 1

Large Room

In a large room there is a method that is utilized to garner the best and most accurate results. This method is called the wagon wheel spoke method. It is called this because the pattern that you perform your base readings, etc. is shaped like wagon wheel spokes when you look at it on paper. Please review Figure 2 for a visual of this protocol.

To gather the readings that you require in a large room you begin in the center. Like the small room, you move to the center of this area

87

you may begin to take your base readings, observations, photographs, etc. from each point of the compass (North, South, East, and West) and return to the entrance from which you began. Begin by moving to the most extreme left as you possibly can. The next step is the tricky part. You probably will not need a compass for this part, but it is good to keep an eye on the furthest point in the direction you are heading. Once you get to that point you need to return on the same "spoke." Once you get back to the entrance you turn slightly to the right and move out in the same pattern as you first did.

Continue this pattern until the entire room has been combed. Once you have completed the wagon wheel spoke method, progress will have definitely been made. This may take some time but it is well worth it to ensure that all readings, measurements, observations, etc. are made. Again, this method is for a more defined and comprehensive coverage of the area.

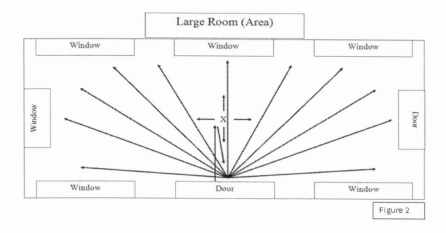

Figure 2

Large Outside Area

A large outside or wooded area is approached in the same way as a large room. The only difference is, you will not move to the center to take readings. The only method to use for this is the wagon wheel spoke method. This method will help you cover more area in your investigation. You will also need to utilize your entire team for this exercise and ensure that they are split and move in opposite directions. Please review Figure 3 for a visual of this protocol.

The first rule I should say is to ensure that you carry with you a compass so that you stay on track. The most important rule to remember is to ensure that you move and investigate in partners. It is very dangerous to be in a large outside area with minimal contact with others.

The command central needs to be established in an area that is preferably on higher ground. This will help the person stationed there to be able to see the teams as they move along. If you cannot put it on higher ground ensure that it is very close to one of the main compass points so that it will be easier to find. Remember that during investigations like these communication is key, so keep in contact to ensure that everyone is okay.

Prior to the investigation you need to plan out this venture. There may be any number of bodies of water around, such as lakes, streams, ponds, etc. Let the investigators know where these areas are so that they can steer clear of them or be prepared when they get there.

Always keep in mind the number one rule of investigations is safety.

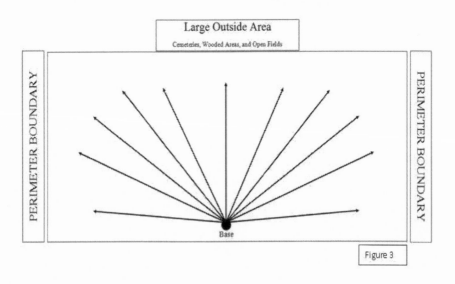

Figure 3

Wooded Areas

During investigations it is a good idea to have in mind a procedure for taking measurements. We have tried many different ways to do this and we feel that the procedures that we are about to present are the best ways to perform taking measurements. We will discuss small and large rooms as well as open and wooded areas.

Let us begin by talking about wooded areas. This includes small or large woods, fields, outdoor lots, etc. Please review Figure 4 for a visual of this protocol. The first step to investigating wooded areas is to establish your perimeter. This is very important to remember especially in large wooded areas. You do not want to wander too far from command central when investigating these types of areas. If it is impossible to establish your perimeter be sure to at least know when to stop and return to command central.

Next you must establish a command central. Command central should be in an area that is clear of trees and brush such as a clearing within the wooded area or on the outskirts of the wooded area. Preferable command central should be on higher ground if at all possible.

After your command central is established the investigations teams must use a compass to ensure that they are on the correct path. The teams must investigate using a pattern perpendicular to the points of the compass. The team will follow this line until they reach the designated perimeter or to the furthest point that they are willing to go. On the return to command central the team takes a left and proceeds to the next nearest compass point and then follow that point using a perpendicular pattern. This will ensure that you will not get lost and will be able to find command central easily.

By using this technique you will be able to cover a lot of ground during the investigation. It also helps keep you safe by not getting lost or worried about where you are. It is always hard to be in a strange place when you do not know where you are going exactly. This will keep you from worrying about getting lost.

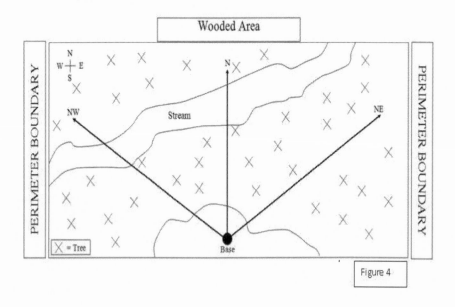

Figure 4

All of the basic investigation steps that are outlined in this section are transferable to investigations of public, commercial, and historic locations. You must use your own judgment as to which protocol would be best suited for the location.

"We all go on the same search, looking to solve the same old mystery. We will not, of course, ever solve it. We will finally inhabit the mystery."

Ray Bradbury

Chapter 5

Paranormal Tech

"It is entirely possible that behind the perception of our senses, worlds are hidden of which we are unaware."

Albert Einstein

The kind of paranormal investigator that you will become is the kind that you truly want to be. The more knowledge you have, the better you will become. The same holds true for the tools of your trade. You can have the best equipment that money can buy but if you don't know how to use it, then these tools will be useless to you. In our research, these tools can often times go where we cannot go and sense what we cannot sense. However, in the end, they can never replace common sense, intelligence, and the human factor. We must always bear in mind that we can only trust our equipment so far and that all equipment has limitations.

I like to begin by classifying the equipment for paranormal investigators use into three distinct categories; Classic Tech, Moderate Tech, and Advanced Tech. I am sure that we can argue over this list for days, however, I cannot argue from a book and I am the author and we will just stick with this list for now. This equipment can be broken down further into more categories, but who has the time. I will go over some items from each category and discuss each item in detail. I know that I will be leaving equipment off of the list but all of the equipment I am going to talk about is equipment that we use and most paranormal investigators use as a whole.

I want to begin by classifying Classic Tech as all of the equipment you will need to have in order to carry out any paranormal investigation. You will be unable to perform a solid investigation without this equipment in hand. This equipment helps us capture and record evidence and without it we only have our word and sadly the world will not accept that alone, especially since there are so many hard core skeptics in the world.

The most important tool in your paranormal tool belt is a piece of basic equipment that is used by millions of people every day in their life and that is a simple pen and paper. I don't know about you but I cannot trust my memory to recount specific instances. That is why it is crucial to write down your experiences during the investigation. If you are unable to write them down while you are investigating, it is a must to do it immediately afterward. Not only does this help you remember what happens but it may be used to verify evidence that you had captured during the investigation.

As paranormal investigators we tend to perform most of our investigations at night and a flashlight is a crucial piece of equipment for this. It is truly a safety consideration more than an investigation tool, but it is still very important none the less. At times paranormal investigators must navigate uneven terrain or they may need to move around in a cluttered space. If you cannot see where you are going you may get hurt and when you are hurt it ruins the investigation for everybody. So, that is really why it is important to stay safe. I am only kidding. Your safety is just a little more important than the investigation. As we move along, a very important feature for the flashlight would be a red or green filtered lens. This ensures that the integrity of the night-vision cameras that you may be using for the investigation is not compromised.

One other safety tool that you must have at your disposal is a two-way radio. These radios keep you in constant contact with your group. Keep in mind, however, that you should never use them unless it is absolutely necessary. When it is necessary just remember that when a group member needs your help you are only a button click away. These radios also help if you have a command central set up with a monitor for static cameras. The investigator stationed at command central may see something interesting on a camera and will need to get someone moved to that location immediately to check things out without ever having to leave their station.

In keeping with the theme of safety that I am apparently on, a first aid kit is an absolute essential piece of equipment. I know that I am including this in a list meant for paranormal investigation equipment, but this item should speak for itself as being important. If someone in your group gets a scratch or falls down, it is good to have first-aid supplies with you to help. Another great tip is to have everyone in your group, or at least someone on your investigation, certified in CPR. The first aid kit is the only piece of equipment that you hope to never have to use, yet you never want to be caught without it.

One important and great device that has been used for many years is the voice recorder. It simply records audio of whatever you have near it. Some investigators are purists and believe that they must use recording devices that use tapes and others are progressionists that think the new digital recording devices are better than or at least equal to the tapes. I for one incorporate the use of digital recording devices. It is not because I am a progressionist, but it is simply due to the ease of data transfer and collection. I can plug the device into my computer and listen to the audio with my audio management software. The largest reason for paranormal investigators to use voice recorders is in hopes of catching an Electronic Voice Phenomena (EVP). EVPs are said to be imprints on the voice recorder that you cannot hear during your investigation. You can only find these when you do your evidence review. Another great reason to have it is to capture Direct Voice Phenomena (DVP). This is when an investigator thinks that they hear something but they are unsure. With a voice recorder you can instantly play back the recording to see if something was captured.

A good camera for still photography is most useful and a camera with night-vision capabilities is an even bigger plus. This piece of equipment can also hinder your investigation. If you do not know how to use your camera properly, you may take pictures that are blurred, out of focus, over-exposed, etc. Also, if you do not understand these concepts you may mistake your improperly taken photos for paranormal phenomena. A good rule to adhere to is what we refer to as the "two for one shot." This simply refers to the practice of snapping two photographs for every one photograph. We also employ snapping photographs at different angles, with the flash, without the flash, etc. One of the biggest mistakes that paranormal investigators around the globe make is simply taking one photograph and attempting to explain a paranormal phenomenon with that one photo. I have seen so many photographs during my time as a paranormal investigator and on so many occasions they can be easily explained and/or duplicated. To be honest, these so called investigators do nothing to help the cause of true paranormal investigators because of their unwillingness to listen. So keep in mind that when you buy a camera, please learn how to use it. Many communities have an adult education center that may provide lessons in photography. These classes are generally inexpensive or, in the best cases, free and they are very informative.

In the same line as a camera, a good hand held video recorder, or camcorder, is great to have on hand. Again, night-vision or full-spectrum capability is almost a requirement for paranormal investigations. If you use a normal camcorder for night time investigations, it will do you no good at all. The camcorder then just turns into a very expensive audio recorder. A camcorder is useful because it will give person reviewing the evidence the investigators personal point-of-view. That is, if you are holding the camcorder properly. The usefulness in the field comes when you think you saw something but are unsure. You can replay the camcorder instantly to see if there was anything there.

Last but not least, of the Classic Tech, is a good side pouch or a photographer's vest. This is a must have item in my opinion. I actually have both at my disposal. I swap from one to the other according to the location and the equipment I want to carry. It is very hard to carry all of the essential investigation tools in your hands or in your pants pockets. With a side pouch or vest you can have easy and quick access to all of your personal investigation equipment.

The next classification I place paranormal investigation equipment in is Moderate Tech. I feel that this is equipment that is not necessary, but it will enhance your investigation greatly. Moderate Tech only gives you more ammunition to perform a great investigation and to enhance your ability to catch any paranormal activity that may be present. I suppose it is safe to say that this equipment is for the more avid paranormal investigator or an established group of investigators. The reason I say that is simply this equipment tends to be more expensive and therefore in order to get your money's worth you must use it.

The number one item on my Moderate Tech list is an Electro-Magnetic Field (EMF) detector. This instrument detects EMF in its surrounding area. The theory behind this particular piece of equipment is that spirits gather the energy around them in an attempt to manifest. This device will aid you in detecting this attempted manifestation and allow the investigator to begin performing tests to try and capture this manifestation on video or photo. You must be careful with this device because there are many objects in a location that may give off an EMF. Before you or any investigator jumps to conclusions you need to ensure that the reading is not coming from one of these devices. It could be a clock radio, wires in the walls, floors, or ceiling, a fuse box or breaker box, a fan, etc. The only drawback that I could find to the EMF meter is that it only works on one wavelength.

To combat the issue of only one wavelength I want to introduce the next device the Tri-Field meter. This device is in the same device family as an EMF detector. However, the difference is it has the capability to sense magnetic, electric, and radio/microwave frequencies. The Tri-Field meter also detects these frequencies on various wavelengths. This gives the investigator a better opportunity to find what may be causing the fluctuation and not immediately lean toward a paranormal explanation. We truly appreciate the Tri-Field meter simply because it is a proven instrument used in scientific as well as manufacturing applications.

One of my personal favorites is the K-II meter. The K-II is nothing more than an EMF meter. The only difference between an EMF meter and a K-II is the fact that it uses Light-Emitting Diodes (LEDs) as the metering indicator. The K-II is also not as accurate as an analog or digital EMF meter, but this tool is not used for its accuracy. These are used for communication purposes. The theory is if a spirit "touches" the K-II it will blink. So, if you ask the spirit a yes or no question it can "touch" the meter to answer your questions. It is good to ask a series of questions and repeat questions to ensure that the meter is just not picking up some anomaly at random.

There is one theory that states when a spirit it trying to manifest it not only manipulates the energy around it but it causes the area of manipulation to become colder. This is what investigators call a "cold spot." In order to truly record a cold spot you must have a temperature meter, thermometer, temperature gun, temperature gage, etc. The best temperature gages have the ability to sweep the room and also have a probe that extends from the unit itself. This probe can be used to find the cold spots while the gage continues to measure the surrounding area. Keep in mind that you must have a baseline reading of the area you are investigating before you decided to use these to detect cold spots.

I had stated in the Classic Tech that an audio recorder is essential for a good investigation. We now have the technology to go a step further. There are audio devices that have a microphone that picks up sound in 360 degrees. This allows the investigator to pick up sound from anywhere in the area they are investigating. These are useful for Direct Voice Phenomenon (DVP) that seems to emanate from a certain direction. With a 360 degree microphone the reviewer may be able to hear the DVP better or clearer. Along with this technology more sophisticated audio recorders are coming to the market, so it is best to research these and find one that suits your needs as a paranormal investigator.

One of the most essential pieces of equipment for the avid paranormal investigator is a DVR with night-vision capable static cameras. You can find DVRs with the capability to record using four static cameras to sixteen. Of course it is according to the location that you are investigating where you set up these cameras and how many you may need. This device also falls back to safety. It allows a team member that is stationed on the monitor to keep track of the teams investigating in the location and to help guide them to areas where you may have spotted something on the monitor. Of course, with this device you need to have a monitor to enable you to see what the DVR is recording and electricity to run them. It is a good idea to keep various size tripods on hand for varying conditions that you may run in to. We always carry tripods from tabletop sized to eight foot (2.5 meters).

Again, in the Classic Tech section I had said that a camera and camcorder were essential to every investigator. If you are a true paranormal investigator, you need to invest in a camera and a camcorder with Infrared (IR) light and Full-Spectrum light capabilities. These devices will assist the investigator with capturing pictures and video in full darkness. Of course, you will need a light source for some of these cameras and camcorders to work properly, but the results are well worth it. Another reason for this particular tech is another theory that states apparitions may manifest in another light spectrum that only these cameras can detect. In my opinion, it is always better to be over-prepared than under-prepared.

One tech that our team actually had success with is called a temperature pod or a temp-pod. This device is set up to detect temperatures plus or minus one degree from a baseline temperature. The temp-pod uses LED indicator lights to let you know that there is a temperature difference in the area you have it set up. We set these up in areas where the client has specified cold spots appearing. That way the temp-pod can alert the team member posted on the monitors that there is a fluctuation and they can send the team to investigate immediately. Just be sure that there is nothing that can cause the temp pod to activate like a breeze from a window or duct work.

We have also have incorporated the use of a REM pod. The REM pod incorporates the use of a telescopic antenna that radiates an

Electro-Magnetic (EM) field around the pod. The pod then senses disturbances in this field and uses LEDs to indicate the level and proximity of the disturbance. Again, the theory of spirits manipulating EM fields to manifest is the basis behind this device. You must be careful when placing this device to ensure that nothing in its surrounding will manipulate the field to give you a false reading.

Now we have come to the best part of all of the equipment, the Advanced Tech. This equipment is really not necessary because if you have an arsenal of Classic and Moderate Tech you will be set for great investigations. Advanced Tech, however, is just plain cool and fun to play with. Another issue with Advanced Tech is it is generally expensive, you need to understand the application, or you may need to train yourself more extensively on the device operation before you use it.

The first piece of Advanced Tech that I am going to introduce is the Geiger counter. These meters have been around for dozens of years. During the arms race between the United States and Russia, Geiger counters were an everyday item in households that had bunkers. These devices are used to detect and measure amounts of radiation. Believe it or not in some instances where individuals think that they are experiencing a paranormal event, they are actually being affected by small doses of radiation. In another theory it is suggested that when spirits try to manifest they can affect the scale of a Geiger counter. So, this piece of equipment may be two-fold for paranormal investigators. On a side note a radon detector would be a great piece of equipment to have for the same reason as the Geiger counter.

A laser blanket is next on my list of Advanced Tech. I know that this does not seem very advanced any longer since you can find them at almost every gas station cash register and they are not very expensive. However, it is how the laser is used that makes me place them in the Advanced Tech section. You have to understand how to set up this piece of equipment with your camera to get the best image possible. That is, knowing where and when to use the laser blanket. If used properly, it may be a very useful tool in your arsenal.

There is a theory that states spirits can use various frequencies to attempt communication. There is a device called a ghost box. This device has actually been around for many years. It uses AM/FM radio frequencies to help you attempt to communicate with spirits. The basic idea is the device creates a white noise by sweeping the radio waves at different speeds. This allows the spirit to communicate with whoever is performing the EVP session. I have had a small amount of success using this device. The only issue is to ensure that what you are hearing is not the voice of the radio waves. That is one mistake that many paranormal investigators make.

As we have stated before, there is a theory that states spirits must use energy to manifest. If a spirit uses energy then another way to test for this is to use a Negative Ion Detector. Basically, negative ions are what buildup to produce static. If you do not believe that static is a buildup of charge, try touching a grounded piece of metal while you have static built up around you. You will see an electrical arc extend from you to the metal and it stings a little. Another thing you must keep in mind is the weather. Bad weather has a massive effect on this device. You must know the settings for your meter at sea level during fair weather. This will give you your average base reading. Ion counts will go up as an electrical storm approaches and the count will significantly go up during a storm. As long as you keep this in mind during your investigation you will be able to use the ion detector to easily find an area that has a large build up and you can go from there with your investigation.

Using this theory we can go further and say that it is possible to help the spirit along with its manifestation. We can also generate negative ions to help the spirit. If you have the skill it is an inexpensive simple device to make. You can also find these for sale in various websites for what I consider to be an inflated price. There are two main things to keep in mind when you are using one of these devices. First, you can no longer use the negative ion detector. Of course, there will be a spike of negative ions in that location because you have just created them. Second, DO NOT TOUCH THE LEADS.

These devices have leads protruding from them and if you touch them they WILL hurt. It is not enough to kill you, of course, but you will know that you have touched them.

There is one fun piece of equipment that is called a Geophone. This device detects movement. You must be careful when using it as it will detect vibration from anything. These devices are mainly used in areas that the investigator will not be traveling to as much or at all. They should be used to detect phantom footsteps in conjunction with a camera and audio recorder. An experienced investigator can keep one on hand and use when movement has been felt. A bed for instance where movement has been reported would be a good place to use the device only after you have experience using it. They can be handy devices, but they can fool an investigator very easily.

There is a device that aids in detecting DVPs called a Parabolic Microphone. This device amplifies all sound around you and most have the capability to use a voice recorder connected straight to the device. I have used one of these devices in a case and have been able to direct investigators to a location because I detected phantom footsteps. It is a great device to use when you are also investigating cryptozoological locations. It gives you a heads up on anything around you.

The last, but definitely not the least, of my list of advanced equipment is the Thermal Imaging Camera. This is the device that most groups drool over to get their hands on. It is included because of the very high price tag that this equipment has. It not only detects differences in temperature, but it gives you an image of the area the sensor is pointed in. So, if there is an anomalous presence it will give you a visual representation of that anomaly even if you cannot see it with your naked eye. This gives the investigator the ability to find areas that cold spots can come from or it gives them a visual representation of the spirit that is causing the cold spot. Either way, this device is definitely one for the true paranormal investigator.

This concludes my list of equipment for paranormal investigation. It is by no means a conclusive list, but it is a list of some of my favorites. There is new equipment being developed all of the time and there is a lot of equipment that I may have left off. I assure you one thing though, if you can obtain all of the equipment that I have laid out in this section you are well on your way to becoming a great paranormal investigator.

"The real problem is not whether machines think but whether men do."

B.F. Skinner

Chapter 6

What Makes an Investigator?

"We don't see things as they are; we see them as we are."

Talmud

We have gone over what it takes to have a successful investigation and now it is time to talk about what takes to make a successful paranormal investigator. You must always remember that the most important tool in your investigation kit is you! A successful investigation always depends on the investigator. You may have all of the best equipment money can buy, but if you do not prepare yourself the investigation will be for naught. In this section I want to discuss all aspects of becoming a successful investigator. You must keep in mind that each aspect is crucial to an investigation.

The number one aspect on any investigators list should be attitude. Attitude is an enormous aspect when dealing with any team of people and with clients. Your attitude will set the pace for an entire investigation. If you have a poor attitude and seem very difficult to deal with, your team will adopt the same attitude. This is generally felt by the client and may cause the client to believe that all paranormal groups are this way. Worse yet they may get uncomfortable with you being there and ask that you leave. A good attitude goes a long way, especially when you are dealing with clients. Sometimes something will happen that may get you upset, but ALWAYS take it away from the clients. Never bicker or argue in front of a client. Also, NEVER undermine the authority figure on an investigation. It is very unprofessional and it will leave the client with second thoughts about this field and its organizations.

Your philosophy is also very important to your investigation. I am not referring to your religious philosophy or your general philosophy of life. I am referring to your philosophy of the paranormal. I have worked with individuals that have absolutely no belief in the paranormal. Their entire premise for being there is to belittle every experience that the client and the team has. Their paranormal philosophy was based on pure skepticism. On the other hand I have worked with individuals that were extreme believers. These individuals always try to explain everything as paranormal, even if it is easily explained. Their paranormal philosophy is pure belief. In this field having a balance of the two philosophies will help you become a better investigator. Believing in the paranormal is important, but you must keep a skeptical yet open mind when it comes down to the investigation.

A very important aspect of a successful investigator is the ability to control your fear. If you are afraid of the dark, you probably should not be a paranormal investigator to begin with. Controlling one's fear is simply understanding what you are afraid of and confronting it with that understanding. If you are in a group that has been together for a long time you will begin to see the older members not getting as excited as the younger members. That is because they are approaching the situation with understanding.

When I was growing up I had always said that I was afraid of the dark. I later come to realize that the dark is not what I was afraid of. It was what was lurking in the dark. When I got older I began to realize that, though evil did lurk in the dark, I was able to face it head on. I then began to investigate the paranormal and my understanding of evil grew. Now, though I know that evils do lurk in the dark and they only want to scare you. So, I can now face them head on with no fear. Point being, I faced my fear and I now understand it. I did not out-grow my fears in anyway, I just decided that I must accept them and learn from them.

The dangers of fearing the darkness and unknown go far beyond your emotional distrust. It goes right in line of your personal safety and the safety of your teammates. If you are frightened very easily and a cat jumps out while you are investigating, you may hurt yourself or your teammate trying to get away. The first safety rule of investigation is never run from anything. This is not only dangerous to you, but your teammate and the client's property. If for whatever reason you do feel uncomfortable, just back out of the area and walk swiftly away. However, a true paranormal investigator never walks away from the darkness. They trudge through the darkest of places in search of answers.

There is also another caveat to controlling your fear and that is being over-zealous. It is okay to be confident in yourself and your abilities, but believing you are in control of every aspect is just as dangerous, if not more dangerous, as being fearful. Not to mention, it is very foolish to believe that you are in control. This is when you may run into a somewhat nasty spirit that wishes you harm. Being over-zealous it may lull you into a false comfort and then strike you when your guard is lowered. ALWAYS have your guard up and understand that you are NEVER in complete control. Spirits attack you in four different ways; physically, mentally, emotionally, and spiritually. If you let your guard down for a moment, an evil spirit can strike at you in any of the four ways.

There was one time that I did let my guard down because I suspected the place we were investigating to harbor nothing more than a residual haunt at most and that was my first mistake. My second mistake was to not prepare for the worst even if it were just a residual haunt. Though I was prepared physically, mentally, and spiritually, I let my emotional guard down and we ran into a rather nasty spirit that night. So, it attacked me emotionally. I began to get depressed and I felt alone, even though I was with another investigator. The effects of this were toned down when I left the area, but I was still affected for almost four days afterward. I have never since let my guard down and I don't want any of you reading this to do the same. Those feelings I had were horrible and they could have been so much worse if I had more guards down.

The next aspect is one that can not only have an effect on you as a paranormal investigator, but it will have an effect on the entire paranormal field as a whole. This aspect is called honesty. We are not only talking about honesty with clients, but we are talking about being honest with yourself as well. The biggest thing to remember is that you will not catch evidence every time you venture out for an investigation. It is not to say that the location is not active but the activity may just simply be settled while you are there. The thing to keep in mind is the fact that paranormal activity is not like a light switch. You cannot simply turn it on and off at will. Some investigators think that if they did not capture anything that the investigation was a failure. This is not true at all! This is when these investigators feel the need to begin manipulating their "evidence" and present false evidence to the client. I can tell you without any hesitation that I abhor this kind of behavior. If I were to catch one of my team members doing this there would be no reprimand, they would be off of the team for good. This is how serious this aspect is to the field of paranormal investigation. I would rather disappoint a client by throwing away a piece of evidence that is on the fringe than present manipulated evidence to them. This not only becomes a lie to the client but it is a lie to the paranormal collective. I know that you have heard the saying "one bad apple ruins the bunch." This most definitely applies here. The paranormal field is already seen a quack pseudo-science and these lies that certain groups bring forth as evidence only push us further back. We need to remember to take a stand and be honest and truthful. It is the only way to bring our field into the future.

The next two aspects for becoming a successful investigator go hand in hand. They are skepticism and belief. Just to reiterate, as paranormal investigators we must always first prove what something is not before we can prove what it is. A true paranormal investigator must keep this in mind when learning this balance. Too much of one and not enough of the other is always a bad combination. For instance, I am a believer in the paranormal but I do not let that belief overshadow my investigations. I always bring just enough skepticism to the investigation to allow me to be un-biased.

The goal of any investigation is to investigate with zero bias. I don't want to seem too skeptical because it will make the client feel belittled or crazy, yet if I seem to find the paranormal in everything it may make the client feel uneasy. These aspects are very hard to teach and even harder to understand, but once you have the grasp of the concept it will become second nature to you.

I seem to always over analyze every situation when I am training a new investigator that is a true believer. I am not trying to steer them away from their belief in the paranormal. I just need them to look at a situation or evidence with a more critical eye. The investigator needs to understand that a certain piece of evidence may eventually be deemed paranormal, but they should not simply direct their thoughts that way until all objective reasoning is used. I simply do not want to jump the broom every time someone sees a shadow in a photograph. I want them to objectively look at it and eliminate all possible scenarios before they decide to present it as evidence.

As an example, I was training an investigator that brought me a photo that had the exact same shadow in the exact same location in every photo they presented it. This investigator brought it to me immediately wanting to present it as evidence. When I told them to look at it again I could see outward disgust because they just knew that it was evidence. I asked them to get out the camera and take several pictures for me. They did this and I immediately noticed how close their finger was to the lens of the camera. I took the camera from them and asked them to watch me as I took a picture. I used the same target for several photos. I took a picture correctly for all but the last one and I slightly put my finger in front of the lens and it made the exact same shadow we had been seeing. The investigator immediately saw the connections and has been more careful ever since. Again, we must always first prove what something is not before we can prove what it is.

On the flip side of this, I also have as difficult of a time trying to train a skeptic. Skeptics feel that everything has an explanation even if they cannot find one. The problem there is they begin to assume things that cannot be proven otherwise. I have also found that these investigators also have a hard time going into an investigation with an un-biased attitude. Sadly, these types of investigators are usually broken when we run into a rather nasty spirit and they are attacked for the first time. They tend to want to discredit it at first, but they eventually concede to the fact of what happened to them was paranormal. Once this happens their eyes seem to open and belief begins to set in and they find that happy medium between skepticism and belief.

The one instance that I remember this happening was when I first began investigating the paranormal. There was an investigator that was a hard core skeptic and we ran into a very nasty spirit on this particular night. This investigator was physically attacked and had to not only leave the house but the premises. That is when their eyes opened and they could see the veil that lies between our world and the unseen. It is sad to imagine that this is how we must break a skeptic, but it is how it needs to be done. That particular investigator stopped investigating for a while but eventually came back with their eyes wide open. They then understood what was meant by a healthy combination of skepticism and belief.

The last aspect I want to present is one that seems to be overlooked in today's electronic society and that is patience. That is something that we must contend with every day as leaders of a paranormal group. Some of our investigators coming in are not very patient. They tend to want instant gratification and if they do not get it they want to move on. As I mentioned earlier, the paranormal is not like a light switch that we can switch on and off anytime we please. Sometimes it takes a lot of sitting and observing in both the investigation and the review of evidence. If you are not patient and observant, you may miss a very important minute detail. That detail may include you watching a hallway and see or hear something in another room. If you have patience you can watch this area and see if there is a pattern to it or if it is random. This may even lead to your next area to investigate but you must remain still, quiet, and observant. If you are constantly moving around and talking then nothing will happen.

Think of game hunters in the woods. These hunters are the best example of patience I can think of. They prepare the area for the hunt and then sit and wait for their game to appear. This is the same principle for paranormal investigations. We prepare for the investigation and then we must sit, wait, and above all be patient.

The very nature of all things paranormal is to stay hidden we must never forget that. It is also the essence of the mysterious and the unknown. This makes our quarry very elusive and that does make us hunters. As good hunters we must seek always the clues and signs of our target and always know as much as possible about our quarry. Those clues or signs can also be trails or patterns that will hopefully tell us the information we need to know and to better understand the nature of what we are seeking and to reach the goal of our quest. We are the truth seekers and the truth is always our quest.

That is why we must seek out the known patterns of the paranormal. Patterns are very important in scientific research. They are a mainstay to experiments as well. To experiment is to probe and that is a foundation of scientific research and how we can of course acquire knowledge. The tools of observation and replication are essential in the use of scientific investigation.
Research should also always include as many related subjects as much as possible, to the main one. For if they are inter related they may also have patterns as well that will link them together.

"The real voyage of discovery consists not in seeking new lands but seeing with new eyes."

Marcel Proust

Chapter 7

The Types of Hauntings

"The forms and the creatures have a purpose. God said, I was Hidden Treasure, and I desired to be known."

Mevlana Jelaluddin Rumi

There are many types of haunting known to paranormal researchers. In this section we are going to list a few of the main types that may be encountered in the field. We want to ensure that all of you have some sort of understanding of each type of haunting before you encounter it. Each type of haunting has various things in common but there is one most basic element that each one contains. All hauntings have a factor of the mysterious.

Elemental Spirits

Elemental spirits are supposedly related to some facets of nature such as earth, fire, water, and air. The entities know as fairies (the Sidhe/Siog), gnomes, elves, leprechauns, brownies, trolls, sprites, banshee, etc. are all thought to be elementals and this also encompasses earth light elementals such as will-o-the-wisps, jack-o-lanterns, corpse lights, and so on. This would also include those beings known as the Jinn. According to mythology these classes of beings were once angels and did not take sides during the war in heaven and since they did not fight against the forces seeking to overthrow God, they too were cast out with the evil "fallen" angels. This explanation is found in the mythology of Ireland, Wales, Scotland, along with a few other cultures. According to some demonologists, this is why they along with the angels that rebelled (demons), are so jealous and hateful of humankind. They were made spiritually lower than man. This hatred is what some would say makes them dangerous and gives them their malevolent side. They also, like their demon counterparts, can take on any form and this explains the many shapes, forms, and kinds of creatures that they can appear as to humans. They are known to inhabit (haunt) ruins, hills, mountain tops, fairy rings, forts, and mounds. It is also noted that they favor strange trees and rock formations, crossroads, woods, caves, and places of the dead. They have often been seen by bodies of water such as rivers, near bridges, and ravines. They are sometimes worshipped and favored in witchcraft and old pagan religions. This too could be another link to their demonic roots. The tell-tale sign to knowing if you are dealing with an elemental spirit is often where they appear and how they appear, as their form is often misleading but one you will have some knowledge of. They will seek always to communicate for dark and deceitful purposes.

Religious and Crisis Apparitions

Crisis apparitions can sometimes be the appearance of a recently deceased relative or very close friend. It may also be the spirit of someone that is in great mortal danger and very close to death. These individuals can make their presence known during times of needed comfort or crisis. They can be there to warn of an impending circumstance of danger or to simply convey a message. We may also find this in cases of religious apparitions. Religious apparitions are ones such as saints, angels, the Virgin Mary, etc. It is thought by demonologists, however, that demonic forces may use these same figures to cause harm and deceive. It is always best to test the situation and know what you are truly dealing with. The spirits of God and goodness never lie and do not create feelings of negativity or unreasonable fear. However, the forces that are evil and negative do want to cause harm and fear. The moral compass inherent in all human kind in its basic form is a good barometer for the testing of these spirits.

Poltergeist

Poltergeist is the German word for 'noisy ghost.' Poltergeist activity is thought by many to be a situation where basic psychic energy of adolescents (especially young girls) causes things to happen and is mistaken for a spirit activity. Some demonologists suspect that this activity could be a demonic manifestation masquerading as poltergeist activity. Other beliefs suspect poltergeist activity to be the work of the Jinn. House blessings have been somewhat successful in this situation and much of the time this incident will slowly diminish with the passage of time. The easiest way to determine poltergeist activity is simply the manipulation of objects and sometimes their disappearance and reappearance. If there is a physical attack of any kind during poltergeist activity, this may be an indicator of a demonic presence as well.

Residual Hauntings

The simplest way to explain a residual haunting is to liken the activity to a reoccurring movie reel. If any person or persons are in the right place at the right time, you might be able to observe this phenomenon. One theory about this type of haunting is that what you are witnessing is not really in your time frame or perhaps even the same dimension. Quite possibly this may be a time event of some sort. The situation, along with the people, animals and objects will never acknowledge your presence. They go about their task without ever acting as though you are there. These are often the types of hauntings that are observed on ancient battlefields and old hospitals, especially wherever traumatic events have taken place. This kind of haunting is usually not dangerous in any way and is a very interesting phenomenon to observe and to research or investigate.

Human Hauntings

Human hauntings are the spirits of the dead who have returned, or in most cases, never left. There have been thousands upon thousands of books and papers written on this subject. This phenomenon crosses all cultural lines and has always fascinated humankind. The jury is still out on this long, long case however. It is thought by some paranormal investigators that most human hauntings are brought about by a human spirit that for one reason or another is bound to a certain place and perhaps a certain time. That theory may hold true. However, some spirits do wander and are lost. Many theorize that although they remain, they often do not linger very long after their death. Some demonologists think that a lot of so called ghosts that are seen are really demons masquerading as the dead. In the true case of human hauntings there will be some kind of communication initiated on the part of investigator and spirit. If you have determined that what you are dealing with is indeed a human spirit and you have determined that the spirit you are dealing with is a wandering, bound, lost or confused entity, then it would seem that the correct thing to do would be to perform what is called a soul rescue or spiritual guidance exercise. This procedure should be performed to allow the spirit closure and peace of some kind. However, you must be very careful and you must understand exactly what you are really dealing with. To this end, a lot of research and study must be made concerning this type of haunting and situation so please proceed with caution.

Inhuman Hauntings

This of course involves an in-depth study of Demonology. To be certain of what you are dealing with in this situation, please refer to the section of this book that outlines the study of the Demonic. Inhuman spirits (demons or evil spirits) of course have never walked this earth as humans. According to Christian Demonologists, the fallen angels who became demons along with the rest of the angels who did not rebel were made spiritually lower than humans. For that reason alone, these evil angels hate us, are jealous of us, and seek our downfall and destruction. According to the Christian Bible and belief, they are the rulers of this present civilization and are thought to be in the background of all facets of our lives. It is also known that these dark forces can sometimes invade our personal lives in what is termed oppression and possession. Most of the time by our lifestyle alone, such as dabbling in Satanic or occult rituals and such, we can advertently or inadvertently open up ourselves to these forces. This is especially the case when our minds have been altered by means of drugs and/or alcohol and also other methods. It should also be noted that these forces can have a controlling influence over animals, objects, and places. It is thought too, that doppelgängers also fall into the area of the demonic. These known entities can be very, very dangerous and if you should encounter or suspect that you are dealing with the Demonic, then it would be advisable to enlist the aid of someone who has had experience with this subject, such as Clergy or a Demonologist.

Shadow People

This type of paranormal encounter is becoming more predominate and seems to occur in many cases that can be linked to the demonic. Leading Demonologists have considered that this is one of the many ways in which demons can manifest themselves. Shadow people or shadow creatures, as they are often called, are shadows that have formed or can form without the use of any type of light as their source. They will appear to be a shadowed outline that is darker than the surrounding darkness and sometimes seem to be wearing some type of hat. These shadows have also often been reported as having red eyes. These things have been known to physically attack people. More often than not, they appear just at the edge of a person's peripheral vision and are rarely seen with a straight on gaze. Amazingly enough, these creatures have also been linked to ufology and general hauntings as well. It is best when dealing with this type of haunting to seek the help of a paranormal investigator who has experience with this entity or perhaps a Demonologist as well.

Strange Creature or Cryptids

This list includes all mythical monsters, Bigfoot, Werewolves, Dogmen, Lake Monsters, Chupacabra , Vampires, ABC's, OOPA's, Mothman, Jersey Devil, Owl man, etc. The many subjects listed under the header of strange creatures or cryptid hauntings deserve their own books. These things have, in the past, been written about many times over. So, what needs to be said here is how to approach this type of paranormal activity. If you are confronted by cases having to do with ABC's (alien big cats) or OOPA'S (out of place animals) you would of course immediately look into whether any animals have recently escaped from private compounds, zoos and circuses. As with werewolf, Bigfoot sighting etc., you must of course look for physical evidence by visiting the location, if at all possible, and interviewing witnesses and documenting your findings. When conducting interviews with an eyewitness, be sure to record the interview on video if you can or at a minimum record them on audio. Make a transcript of the interview along with notes of your thoughts and impressions on the eyewitness sighting. It is important that you do that as soon as possible, because your memory can sometimes play tricks with your mind over time. It is also important to take as many photos, videos, emf readings, and audio recordings as possible. The more fishing poles that you have in the water the more fish that may be caught. If you can, it would of course be good to stake out the location for your own sighting. It is thought by many paranormal researchers that when it comes to this type of haunting that there could be evidence of an interaction with a possible portal of some kind. This is good to keep in mind in case you should see some evidence of this during your investigation. Just as a reminder, the many basic steps of a paranormal investigation hold true for this type of case as well.

Ghost Lights

This list includes energy orbs, intelligent orbs, dust/water orbs, etc. Okay, one more time just for the record, 99.9% of all orbs seen and captured on film and video are dust motes and water droplets in the surrounding atmosphere. They are enhanced by photographic flash and infra-red light, especially when using digital technology. I have heard so called paranormal investigators say that this is a naturally occurring phenomenon and that each orb has a face and that the different colors mean various things. Simply put, they do not. These individuals are reading something into nothing by saying that these orbs are spirit manifestations. Again, they are not. When you put forth an answer simply because that's the answer you want, then you are completely ignoring the real truth of the matter. This simply makes you look like a fool. With that being said, let us turn our attention to what is a true unknown when you are talking about real "ghost" lights. Energy orbs are a different subject altogether, as their properties are related to known similarities of energy that may be termed spiritual energy. They are reported in paranormal activity as appearing sometimes as small bubbles of energy that can burst like a bubble with an auditory pop. However, these types of orbs are extremely rare and may be related to some sort of unknown natural sources. True ghost lights noted in the past are different in property to energy orbs, as they are soundless and do not burst. They sometimes move with an observable intelligence, as they can go around objects or back off from obstacles. Then too there are earth lights such as the Min Min lights in Australia, the Marfo lights of Texas, the Brown Mountain lights of North Carolina, and so on.

There are even some lights of this kind that are associated with haunted activity, such as the Mako light of the Carolinas that reportedly is carried as a lantern light by the ghost of a headless railroad brakeman. The basics of paranormal investigation should be carried out while doing this type of case and, as always, research as much as possible.

High Strangeness

These encounters are considered to be UFOs/USOs, Black Helicopters, Crop Circles, Alien Abduction, Cattle Mutilation, Men in Black, Secret Underground Bases, Strange Sights/Sound Occurrences, Black Eyed Kids (BEK), Underground Earth Noises, etc. All of the previously mentioned subjects fall under the heading of "High Strangeness." There are even a large percentage of Bigfoot sightings that correlate with UFO reports. When confronted by these types of paranormal activity and reports, the true investigator must do all in his power to get to the heart of the matter and uncover the truth, wherever it may lie. If there are clandestine actions being carried out or cover ups being initiated, then that too must be carefully evaluated. Witnesses must be interviewed, documentation must be carried out, and a physical investigation and observation must be performed if possible. Always remember to be careful, as you are definitely treading in deep and murky waters and into a subject matter that may even grow stranger with time. The one thing that I can say about this type of encounter is simply that it cannot be put down once it is picked up.

Witchcraft /Occult/Satanic Hauntings

These types of hauntings are perpendicular to a location. Although in cases of a curse or hex, they can attach to people and follow where ever they may go. It is thought by many researchers that one of the main goals of black witchcraft and Satanic /dark occult activity, is that these sects continually work to open doorways and portals to allow the manifestation of demonic power, for the use of the participants. When this is accomplished, rarely are those doorways ever closed, whether intentional or not. Wherever these rituals are performed the demonic or evil influence will linger and remain. You may never know what evil things may have been carried out in a specific location, but more often than not, you will see the factors of fallout associated with these actions. The sad reality is that this fallout can badly affect those who must live in close proximity to these areas, that were stained by past occult activity. When such portals are supposedly opened anything can come through and these types of situations should only be handled by skilled paranormal investigators and Demonologists. This rule also applies to any type of fallout brought forth by curses, hexes, spells, and demonic contracts. Any attachment of evil, must only be handled by individuals that have the knowledge to work with this type of haunting.

Tricksters-Shapeshifters

This category falls under the auspices of the Jinn , Loki, Wendigo and the skin-walker. These types of hauntings cross all cultures around the world. If you should ever suspect that you are confronted by this type of haunting your best course of action may be to seek help from those who know exactly how to deal with these entities. Research is absolutely required to understand more about these types of hauntings. Be warned that most people who do know of these things don't like to talk about them or acknowledge them. These individuals truly believe that to mention them or give them any kind of attention would bring them to you and cause terrible retribution. Skin-walkers in particular are associated with dark witchcraft practices by the Native-Americans and they believe that these entities are to be avoided at all costs. The Power of the Jinn is feared throughout the eastern world as well, so they are seldom mentioned by these people. Ensure you perform as much research as possible before you even attempt any kind of investigation into these entities.

Portals, Gateways, Doorways, and Vortices

There is a theory that many hold as truth and that is, that there are time and space dimensional shifts, lost time, Dead Zones, etc. It is said that some of the most likely places to find portals are at crossroads, mountain tops, hills unusual trees and rock formations, forests, graveyards, and sacred places such as the ruins of old abbeys. It is also thought that portals may appear anywhere or any time. Portals are thought to exist especially where Ley lines (Earth Energy Lines) intersect. It is also theorized that where these Ley lines run, there can be a higher incident of paranormal happenings. It is possible that a portal and a vortex may be two different things entirely. A portal may be an inter-dimensional type opening and a vortex may be more of a hole in space and time itself. The aspects of portal and vortexes can possibly be explained by quantum physics. UFOs and strange creatures have been witnessed by some to enter and exit portals and in the presence of vortexes and portals there can be a distortion of space and time as well as inter-dimensional shift. Lost Time episodes are also reported around portals and vortices. It is theorized that the presence of portals and vortices may cause a slight shift the magnetic fields affecting instruments such as EMF detectors and compasses. There is another instance reported concerning portals and gateways that are opened and invoked by the use of the black arts. These openings are used to call forth demons and obtain use of their power. If you think you have a case involving portals and doorways, it is a good idea to do as much research as possible on this subject before you proceed to investigate. But be warned, not a lot of knowledge exists on these things, only a few case histories. So proceed only with extreme caution.

"What I thought was unreal now, for me, seems in some ways to be more real than what I think to be real, which seems now to be unreal."

Fred Alan Wolf

Chapter 8

Review and Use of Evidence

"Always remember that when you have committed yourself to an action, then the whole cosmos will conspire to help you. The keyword is commitment."

Mark Hedsel

Every investigator and investigation team seems to have their own technique for reviewing evidence. I really do not want to spend a lot of time on this subject, but it is the most crucial part of any investigation. Without the review, an investigation will have only been for entertainment. This, as we have already discussed, is not why we are in paranormal investigation and this is not what this book is about. Not that getting entertainment from an investigation is wrong, but it is not the primary objective.

I personally find it exhilarating to listen to a long track of audio and out of nowhere hear something that should not be there, or to search a long series of photos and find that one with something odd standing out, or, better yet, while you scan that video and find something creeping along the screen.

These next few steps we are going to go over are very important to remember. It will only help you during the long periods of time that you will be sitting and listening or watching. The first thing to keep in mind is the amount of evidence that you need to cover. If you had an eight hour investigation and used three video cameras and four audio devices, that is 56 hours of real time video and audio you must go over. This doesn't include and video, audio, or photos that you captured while using personal\mobile equipment. It is nice when you are able to distribute the evidence among the members of the group. You may also be able to find someone that may not want to investigate but still wishes to help the team. These individuals are very good to have handy when a lot of review is necessary. This not only cuts down on the time it takes to review, but you may also have time for a second review of the evidence to ensure that you have found something. A second review is most beneficial to a team that wants to give the client the best service possible.

Let us first discuss what you should do before any kind of evidence review. Before any review the most important aspect to keep in mind is that you must be well rested. This will ensure that your focus is sharp and you remain alert during your first review session. When you chose a place to review, it needs to be a quiet secluded area with no distractions. It is okay to have a snack or a drink with you, but keep in mind if you are reviewing video you must keep your eyes on the screen the entire time. If you need to look away from the screen, you should first pause the video. Another thing to keep in mind is NO ALCOHOL during the review.

Video review is sort of an art with trial and error set up. When reviewing video you need to set up in an area that you can watch the entire screen. If you have a smaller screen you need to set up closer to the screen, however, if you have a large screen, you need to sit further away from it. The best example I have for this is an average computer screen is around 16" and if you set up at a computer desk or a kitchen table this distance should be about right.

Reviewing static camera video is almost like watching paint dry because you are staring at the same location the entire time, but it allows you to easily catch any anomalies that happen in the view of the camera. It is best to watch the screen for about 10-20 minute intervals and then pause and give your eyes a rest. This reduces the strain on your eyes and it helps to keep your attention focused on finding evidence. This is especially important to remember when you have many hours of video to review. The break only needs to be a few minute. Just long enough to go to the restroom or grab yourself a fresh snack. The important thing to remember is your eye health, along with your sanity.

Next is reviewing audio. Never review audio when there are other distractions available. When you review audio that is what you need to concentrate on. You will need a quiet room with no television, books, computer, tablet, or any other form of visual distraction. I know that this seems odd, but when you are attempting to concentrate on something that is completely auditory, you need that to be your complete focus. Our minds create an automatic filter for background noise when we are not fully concentrating on the audio and this may cause you to miss something. An example of needing to concentrate is when you are travelling in your car and you are trying to find a location. What is the first thing that you do? You turn down the volume on your radio or you turn the radio off. This is your brains way of saying that it needs to concentrate on the task at hand. This applies to audio review as well. When you begin to read a book or surf the internet, your brain shuts off the background noise and you cannot concentrate of the review.

Now with that said, I am going to tell you a secret that I have found that works wonders. I do use my computer when I am reviewing my audio. I know that I said you need to concentrate on the audio with no visual stimulus distracting you, but I use a sound editor to accompany my review. A sound editor gives you a visual representation of what you are listening to. It will also give you a visual when you think you may have heard something. It is also easier to isolate and replay with a sound editor. I like to think that it is two of your senses working together for one cause, so it makes the review much better.

The third thing to remember while reviewing audio is to have a good set of headphones. I do not suggest speakers simply due to the ambient noise in the room you are in. Also, do not use noise reducing headphones as they may reduce the quality of the sound of any EVP that may be there. I know that sounds counter-intuitive, but noise cancelling earphones makes the audio clearer therefore reducing the ability of listening for the sounds in the background. I have tried many different kinds of headphones over the years. I have found that the most comfortable and the ones that have the clearest sound are studio headphones. They fit comfortably on your head and the sound is generally better. There is no need to find the top of the line headphones, but you do want to invest in a pair that will give you the best chance of success when reviewing audio.

Reviewing photographs is an art all its own. There are so many groups out there that give into the idea of orbs. There are even different classifications and descriptions of these orbs. In our group we do not give a lot of stock to photographs of orbs. They can be too easily re-created. The best advice I can give someone that wants to review photographs is to do a lot of research on photography. This will give you an understanding of lighting, exposure, focus, angles, etc. There is so much detail that you can learn when looking at photographs. I am going to explain how we review them, but it will be up to you to learn what to look for. Remember, research is what turns a good paranormal investigator into a great one.

When doing a photograph review, I first like to pull up all of the photographs on my computer screen and do a general sweep of all of them. I try to find ones where something may jump out at me. If I do find one I pull it up and enlarge the photograph to the size of the computer screen. This will allow me to find if there is an explanation of the oddity. If there is I make sure that I write it down and what the explanation is and move on. If after the initial sweep I find nothing, I go through each photograph one by one.

Once I have the photograph on the screen I start in the top left corner and move my eyes all around the photograph in a clock-wise motion and spiral around until I reach the center. This will allow me to find anything that may be hidden in the background of the photograph. I then zoom in and begin doing the same thing I start at the top left corner and spiral the photograph around until I reach the center. The last thing I do is zoom out and look at the entire photograph. This ensures that every photograph has been thoroughly checked and re-checked. Now if the photograph is dark you may want to lighten the color slightly to ensure that you are able to see everything clearly.

Another trick that I have learned that can be most beneficial is filtering the colors in the photograph or creating a negative of the photograph. By doing this, the images in the photograph may become clearer or more prominent. This will give you a better view as you study the photograph. The one thing to keep in mind is to be extremely careful of matrixing. Your mind always tries to create familiar images in the things we look at. That is why a lot of people see Elvis in their toast.

Your job as a paranormal investigator is to ensure that all of your evidence is looked at and inspected with the upmost care. Every client deserves to have all of the evidence captured at their location reviewed properly and thoroughly. If you do not review the evidence with the same fervor that you captured it, you may as well quit investigating and find something else to do. Evidence review IS the most important part of ANY investigation.

"I shall not commit the fashionable stupidity of regarding everything I cannot explain as a fraud."

Carl Gustav Jung

Chapter 9

The Field of Paranormal Study

"There are two ways to be fooled. One is to believe what isn't true; the other is to refuse to believe what is true."

Soren Kierkegaard

The field of the paranormal is a most fascinating and addictive field to become involved in. Though we have had many years in the field, Dennis with more than forty years and Brandon with ten years, it is still as fresh to us as the first day we became interested in the paranormal. As we have stated elsewhere in this book, there are no true experts in the field of the paranormal; there are only those that have had more experience than others, but that holds true with many facets of life.

The one thing that we hope to pass along by offering this book to everyone is the simple fact that the more you put in to this field the more you will get out of it. This falls in line with many things in life, especially study. Dennis has commented at times that his study of the paranormal has closely approached an obsession. However, this obsession is the good kind, in a way. We believe that the more you love the subject you are studying, the more meaning it will have for you. In Dennis' case, he has always loved the mysteries of the world and the secrets they may contain. Dennis often reminds us of the many, many hours that he has spent, in the old days, in the reference rooms of libraries jotting down the information that he needed. Fortunately now, we all have a great resource and tool that gives us access to the libraries of the world at our fingertips and that is the internet. The reference rooms of many libraries are now at our disposal in our homes and even on our phones. That, to us, is a remarkable thing. That is also why we say in this book, that your most basic tool is to accumulate as much knowledge as possible about the paranormal as you can. So, we cannot stress enough...read, read, and read more. Study as much as you can of the many stories, case histories, and sources of the paranormal as possible. Study the founders of the field that we started with, such as Charles Fort, Ed and Lorraine Warren, Hans Holtzer, John Keel, etc. There are also some truly fine "new" talents out there as well. Talents such as Barry Fitzgerald, Nic Redfern, Dustin Pari, Bruce Colville, and Stephen Wagner, just to name a few.

That brings us to our take on the field of the paranormal. We know that the paranormal encompasses so much more than just ghosts or spirits. The true paranormal investigator wants to uncover all of the mysteries of the world, not just hunt for ghosts and spirits. Though these subjects are very important to our work, we must also keep in mind that there are still greater mysteries out there that must be investigated as well, such as cryptids, UFO's, time anomalies, possible portals and so much more. We should never pigeon hole ourselves into believing that ghosts and spirits are the only mystery that is worth solving or that they are the beginning and the end of the paranormal field...they are definitely not.

This field of study is so much more and it is ever growing. That is why as researchers we must always seek a communication and a rapport with our fellow colleagues. What we are speaking of is what our community calls Paranormal Unity. With Paranormal Unity we do not have to agree on methods, ideologies, best practices, etc. We only must understand that we are all working toward the same goal and that we must all come together from time to time and help one another in our search for the unknown. The transference of evidence and possible patterns noted in a basic scientific way are possible clues at times to the answers we may seek. That line of communication is very essential and important to us always as true researchers and investigators and must remain open to us. Research without investigation and investigation without research is truly a dead end. You really can't have one without the other as they are in a way, one and the same. It is very important to always remember this and keep it in mind.

There are of course many ways to investigate the paranormal, but please bear in mind, that some ways are better than others in their outcome. In this book we have offered you what we consider to be one of those better ways and it has, for us, been most beneficial and it has been found to, without a doubt, work for us. We, like many others in this field, are always seeking the best way to better ourselves and that is how it should always be.

The supernatural and the unknown have our number and they do call often. As long as we have the ability we will continue to answer that call. We hope that it will call for you as well and that it will be as rewarding for you as it has been for us.

So in the end let us say that if you are just starting out or if you have ten, twenty, or even fifty years in this field, we are all brothers and sisters of a new family. We truly are kindred spirits. We are not just in this for the thrill, for fame, money or glory. No, we are the truth seekers, we are the explorers at the threshold of a new science and that is indeed something to be truly proud of. Once you have experienced a true taste of the paranormal it will change your entire outlook and give you a new handle on the universe and to that, all we can say is, welcome to the brotherhood...

"I will never let you go into the unknown alone."

Bram Stoker

The Ten Basic Rules of Paranormal Investigation

1. Never ever investigate alone.

2. The safety and security of you and your team is paramount!

3. The client, if there is one, along with the integrity of your professionalism, comes only a close second to the safety and security of the team.

4. No matter how curious you are, NEVER break the law, under ANY circumstances!

5. When investigating the supernatural and the unknown, one must always walk a fine line of skepticism and belief. It is most important to always keep a skeptical eye. However, it is just as important to keep an open mind.

6. Just because there is no activity at the time you investigate, doesn't mean that there is no activity at all.

7. The absolute truth of the matter is what you must always seek. It does not matter how unpopular, improbable, or impossible it may seem to be.

8. If in doubt throw it out. Never present evidence that is not solid and pronounced. If you have to squint to find it or strain to hear it, it is not worth presenting.

9. In the true field of paranormal research and study there are no experts. There are only those who have had more experience than others, but all who take up this study must always remain students of it.

10. Once paranormal activity takes place at a location, it is very reasonable that there can be a re-occurrence of paranormal activity in that same location. So, it is without a doubt that location should be held in accordance with future re-investigation.

The Study of the Demonic

Ephesians 6: 12 – 13 (KJV)

12 For we wrestle not against flesh and blood, but against principalities, against powers, against the rulers of the darkness of this world, against spiritual wickedness in high places.

13 Wherefore take unto you the whole armor of God that ye may be able to withstand in the evil day, and having done all, to stand.

The Signs of Possible Demonic Influence and Inhabitation

The presence of people, places, animals, objects and situations associated with possible demonic infestation or interference

The constant feeling of being watched

The smell of sulfur (brimstone) something burning, decaying flesh and other intense odors without a known source

The activity of shadows without a light source

The sensation of intense depression

The feeling of being out of time and place or something not feeling right

The feeling of unusual coldness and a negative void feeling

Cold spots that move and follow

Hearing strange and unusual sounds

Having your name called without a source

The presence and report of the accumulation of strange animals and insects

Strange and unusual manifestation of objects and people

The presence of an unusual number of toads and reptiles

Bad and depressing dreams associated with the place or situation

Unusual lights (ghost lights-dirty lights-will: o the wisps, corpse candles etc.)

The strange appearance of unusual stains and blood stains

Out of place creatures and objects that should not be there

Words and whispering without a known source

The presence and symbols of snakes, the occult, the Satanic and witchcraft

Strange and unusual rock, wood, and pattern formations

Moving and stationary shadows in mass or outlined shapes that have no light source and are mostly always at the border of perceptual sight

Screams and laughter that have no known source

Unusual wind and weather anomalies

Areas of unusual and unaccountable darkness and shadows

The strange actions and reactions of children and animals

Known places of murder, suicide, trauma, and satanic activity

Tunnels and natural or manmade caves are also supposedly demonic habitation sites along with woods, hilltops, hill mounds and fairy trees and rings

Strange and unusual electrical or technical interference

Exhibiting temporary physical and mental sickness or physical discomfort

The occurrence of paranormal and strange unexplainable activity between the hours of midnight and 4 AM, which are known as the demonic hours

Mirrors, darkened mirrors and crossed mirrors are said to be used by the demonic as well as the supposed manipulation of tarot cards, Ouija boards etc.

As well as anything that can alter the conscious and will of the mind

Deserted roads and places such as graveyards ruined houses and destroyed

Churches, Mountain tops, bridges, cliffs, slaughter houses, mortuaries and places of the dead as well as crossroads are supposedly known places said to be haunted by demons and baleful spirits

Elemental forces of nature can also be used and manipulated by the demonic

Like wild dogs, demons are said to have the pack mentality

The Signs of Possible Demonic Oppression

Unaccountable bruises, marks, scratches and also bite marks (scratches will most often appear in sets of three)

Neglect of personal appearance and hygiene

A worried and depressed nature

An almost constant feeling of being watched

Strange coincidences and paranormal activity (especially around the hours of 2, 3, and 4 am)

Strange whispers, messages and communications

Bad and violent type dreams of blood and death

Seeing shadows and darkness where none should exist

Feelings of death and doom and impending destruction

Seeking to alter the conscious and will of the mind

Unusual illness and withdrawal from society

Strange fascination with death and places of the dead

Restlessness and insomnia especially around 3AM

Hearing voices and hearing your name called

Hearing screams or growls that have no source

The strange smell of sulfur, the smell of decaying flesh and the smell of something burning which has no known source

Intense reaction to or increase in paranormal activity in the presence of religious objects Or the mention of religious names, prayers and symbols and also a strong negative reaction to holy water, the holy wafer, blessed crosses and salt

Physical and mental sickness may often accompany these indicators

The Signs of Possible Demonic Possession

Complete change of character

Unnatural Temper flares and rage

Filthy language they did not use before

Unaccountable bruises, marks, scratches and also bite marks
(scratches will often appear in sets of three and can sometimes spell
out words and or occult symbols)

Strange animal like behavior and the presence of animal smells and
sounds supernatural activity surrounding the subject (incidents of
this nature may often appear at or around the hours of 2, 3, and 4 am)

*** The following are a few of the markers that may also be present.**

The eyes can also appear to go dark and or be completely black in
nature

Speaking in a different voice other than their own

Using a language unknown to them

Memory lapses and lost time

Seeing shadows and darkness where none exists

Isolation from family and friends

Fascination with dangerous animals and objects

Unnatural interest in things of a demonic and evil nature

Tendency to become easily obsessed

Intense hatred of all things Godly and religious

Intense fear of all religious objects

Engaging in filthy and bizarre habits

Neglect of personal appearance and hygiene

Silent and uncommunicative

Highly destructive and violent behavior

Exhibiting a Self destructive nature

An intense and drastic hatred, fear or pain from the application of holy water, salt, the holy wafer and also the application of blessed crosses or prayer cloths, the reading of the Holy Scriptures or prayers and blessings

A drop or decline in mental efficiency

Intense hatred of people and animals

Unnatural emotions and laughter

Unusual manifestation of insects and animals

Unnatural knowledge...especially of future and past events

Restlessness and insomnia especially around 3AM

The strange smell of sulfur, the smell of decaying flesh and the smell of something burning which has no known source

Intense reaction to or increase in paranormal activity in the presence of religious objects or an intense hatred at the mention of religious names, prayers and symbols and at the mention of Jesus Christ and any reference to the holy trinity

A drastic change in their normal perception

Physical and mental sickness may often accompany these indicators

Five or more of these markers may warrant investigation.

Ten or more may possibly lead to a definite conclusion on the presence of Demonic Influences.

Please note

If you are using items for protection and detection, these items must be blessed. These items may include things such as crosses, prayer cloths, holy water, olive oil, sea salt, rosaries, garlic salt, bibles, a holy wafer, and so on.

About Curses and Spells

Curses, spells, and hexes are said to be fueled by demonic forces and like all evil influences they can grow in power by giving them attention. They also find their substance in the power of belief. It is thought by many experts of Demonology that in order for a curse or a spell to work, then whoever the spell caster is, he or she must enter into a demonic contract to activate the power of darkness and evil that must carry out the actions of the curse or spell. That is very much in line with the old belief that if you bargain with the Devil he will always want something in return, which is usually your immortal soul. A contract with a Demon is very, very hard to break but it can be done. It requires for the most part a powerful spiritual battle. It is best to avoid this problem by never engaging the forces of darkness in any kind of agreements.

Definitions

Angel

In Christian belief angels are the celestial attendants to God. They are beings that existed before the time of man. Their power is mighty but they only exist to ensure God's will is exercised. They are the intermediaries between God and humans. Angels, Holy and Fallen, are a spiritual class of being that was created lower than that of men. Angels are used to rescue, guard, protect, deliver messages from God, and to carry out God's will to name a few. One class of Angels that most people are familiar with is the Guardian Angel. They are your personal Angel and they cannot help anyone else, only you.

There are also nine different levels of angels. Below the Angels are ranked in order, 1 being highest rank to 9 being the lowest rank:

1. Seraphim
2. Cherubim (plural of Cherub)
3. Thrones
4. Dominions or Dominations
5. Virtues
6. Powers
7. Principalities
8. Archangels
9. Angels

The Seven Archangels of Heaven

1. Gabriel
2. Michael
3. Raphael
4. Uriel
5. Raguel
6. Remiel
7. Saraqael

Anomaly

An anomaly is an event that cannot be explained using normal thought processes or investigation techniques. In paranormal investigation the term is used when an investigator is unsure what to call the event but is not confident enough to say that it is paranormal.

Apparition

This is the holy grail of paranormal investigating and ghost hunting. It is the sudden appearance or manifestation of a ghostly or shadowy figure. It is said to be the spirit of a human or animal. The most basic definition of an apparition is simply a ghost. *See also Manifest*

Ball Lightning

This is a very rare phenomenon in which lightning can be seen as a glowing sphere. It can last anywhere from a few seconds to several minutes. The glowing ball can be seen in a variety of colors and is accompanied by a hissing sound and the smell of Ozone. This phenomenon generally occurs at ground level during thunderstorms, these spheres are thought to consist of ionized gas. As a general rule ball lightning is harmless, however, it has been known to cause damage by burning or melting objects. Ball lightning has also been known to pass through solid objects and walls. Sadly, science has yet to recreate this phenomenon and has obscenely dismissed it as false.

Cold Spot

A small area within a space that is discernibly colder (10 to 15 °F difference) than the surrounding area that has no natural or logical explanation of its origin. A cold spot is said to be an entity or spirit drawing the surrounding energy in an attempt to manifest.

Cryptozoology

Cryptozoology is the study of creatures that are mythical, presumed extinct, or unverified.

Debunk

This is a simple term for the natural or logical explanation of what was considered to be a paranormal or anomalous event.

Demon

A demon is simply an evil spirit or entity. The contemporary Christian belief is that they are fallen angels that decided to join Lucifer in the rebellion against heaven. Demons exist to hate humans and humanity. There are various levels or ranks of demons. If you had to put it into a category, it is much like a military ranking. Each demon has its specialty and its limitations. The higher the level or rank of the demon, the more powerful it is and the more difficult it is to rid yourself of it.

The Seven Princes of Hell

1. Lucifer – Pride
2. Mammon – Greed
3. Asmodeus – Lust
4. Satan – Wrath
5. Beelzebub (Also called Baal) – Gluttony
6. Leviathan – Envy
7. Belphegor – Vanity and Sloth

Demonologist

This is a person that actively studies and pursues demons or any non-human entity in a scholarly fashion in order to help people. Demonologists are generally sanctified by a religious body to perform rituals of spiritual cleansings, blessings, and in extreme cases exorcisms.

* **We do not suggest that anyone pursue this path unless you are very serious and committed. Demons are very dangerous beings and must be treated as so.**

Demonology

Demonology is simply the study of and the understanding of Demons. Understand that this is in no fashion a worship of demons. You must first understand your enemy before you may battle your enemy.

Ectoplasm

Ectoplasm is thought to be a substance that is left behind when a spirit or entity attempts to manifest. It looks like fog with a consistency of a spider's web. The sad truth is that no one has ever been able to collect this substance for scientific analysis, so we can only say that this substance is theoretical.

Electro-Magnetic Field (EMF)

EMF is said to be present when a spirit or entity is attempting to manifest. The theory is as it attempts to pull the energy from the surrounding area a magnetic field is created. EMF without a traceable source may also be an indicator of a possible portal or vortex. EMF is found in nature and must be careful that it is not a natural substance. EMF can also be generated by manmade appliances. The sources should be checked prior to an investigation.

Exorcism

Exorcism is the religious act and/or ceremony of casting out and ridding a place, person, or animal of demons and evil spirits. It may also be seen as an act of religious faith and duty. It is most always accomplished by the action of priests, clergy, and/or church sanctioned demonologists. Exorcisms have been known to continue for months at a time and are also considered a form of spiritual warfare.

Fear Cage

A Fear Cage is a confined space such as a closet, hallway, basement area, etc. that has a concentration of EMF in that area. The Fear Cage is completed when someone sensitive to EMF begins to feel anxiety, paranoia, or fear while in the area. When they leave this area the feelings subside.

Ghost Hunting

Ghost hunting is exactly what it says. It is act of seeking paranormal events for sport and excitement. These individuals get together for nothing more than socializing. They have no interest in the advancement of the paranormal field.

Haunted

To be haunted means that a location has been verified to have spiritual or paranormal activity.

Influence (Demonic)

Demonic influence is as deadly and impacting as possession and oppression. It also has an added element of quiet and unobtrusively dangerous deceit. It is thought by many demonologists that this influence may run throughout many aspects of this world and our lives and that they are unknown to us in many ways. When it reaches the point when this influence is noticeable it is then at its most damaging and dangerous state. This influence pushes us to commit acts of evil and self destruction and is contrary in many ways to the basic moral makeup of humankind. It is thought by many that this influence corrupts the very nature of the human spirit as well.

Infrared Light (IR)

Infrared (IR) light is light from the lower end of the electromagnetic wave spectrum. This means that the wave has a long wave length and a low frequency. IR light is not visible to the human eye. We can only see IR light using special equipment.

Intelligent Haunting

This is a location that has a spirit that interacts with an individual that lives, works, or is passing through a location.

Investigation

Investigation is an inquiry into an event and or situation. It is also a study into a subject as well and this study is also known as research. This is a vital and absolute part of any investigative process, just as complete and unbiased review at the conclusion of any investigation is an absolute necessity.

Manifest

This is the act of a spirit appearing or attempting to appear in the physical world. This happens by means of shadows, partial figures, or full figures.

Matrixing

This is a phenomenon of the mind. Our minds need to make sense of what it sees and will use relation to other objects in order to do so. An example of this is when people find Elvis in their toast. It is only a darker mark, but your mind makes a connection with the dark spot and Elvis. This is a common downfall to paranormal investigators.

Metaphysics

Metaphysics is defined as the branch of philosophy that treats of first principles, includes ontology (nature of being), cosmology (origin of the universe), and is intimately connected to epistemology (origin, nature, methods, and limits of human knowledge). Metaphysics has steered away from a philosophical ponderance to what is considered to be New Age Enlightenment. Most Metaphysical paranormal investigations include, but is not limited to, dowsing, the use of psychics/mediums, the use of Ouija boards, séances, etc.

*   **We do not say that these methods do not produce results, but these   methods are considered dangerous by CSPRI Inc and are not condoned.**

Oppression (Demonic)

Demonic oppression is the state of being attacked by a demon or demons and the overt and covert interaction of demonic influence in many different levels in a person's life and situation. Demonic oppression can be in the form of a very subtle influence or an outright attack of a physical, mental and/or spiritual nature. Oppression is considered by some to be the stepping stone to possession.

Orb

Orbs are a controversial subject among paranormal investigators. Orbs are considered to be the spirit of a deceased person that is in the form of a small ball of light. There are many viable explanations for orbs captured on photographs. It can be dust, snow, rain, moister in the air, fog, breath, insects, lens flare, reflections, etc. The picture of a true orb would be a ball of light where the emanation is generated at the core of the orb or from outside in. Each paranormal group has their own opinion of orbs and it remains to this day a controversial subject.

*   **CSPRI Inc does not employ the use of orbs as a viable paranormal phenomenon. There are too many variables that can be explained to consider this as paranormal evidence.**

Ouija Board

This is a device that is used to communicate with spirits. It is a board that has numbers, letters, and other symbols printed on it. A Séance is generally performed with the Ouija board. The participants each touch the planchette and ask questions to the spirits. The planchette is then supposed to move on its own accord and use the numbers, letters, and symbols to answer the questions of the participants. A side effect that amateur users are unaware of is the fact that using the Ouija board may cause a gateway to open that will allow terrible things to cross over. The simple truth is if you don't want these things to haunt you, then DO NOT USE THE OUIJA BOARD.

Paranormal

This word translates to "beyond the normal." Paranormal encompasses everything that may seem out of the normal range of being and cannot be explained using conventional knowledge or reasoning.

Paranormal Investigating

Paranormal investigation is going to a location that has known activity and gathering data to prove or debunk the activity. The paranormal investigator also has an obligation to help the client to the best of their ability.

Poltergeist

The poltergeist phenomena may be one of the most studied and least understood of all paranormal phenomena. As it relates to paranormal studies, there are different opinions as to whether or not a poltergeist is related to ghostly activity at all. Let us first look at the definition. The term poltergeist is a compound of the German verb polter – 'to make a noise by knocking or tumbling about, to knock or rattle, to scold or blister'. The noun geist is ghost. So, it basically means a noisy ghost.

As the name suggests, poltergeist disturbances usually feature and may begin with some kind of noise, varying from rapping, knocking, scratching sounds, rumbling noises or banging sounds. Other typical noises include moans, screams, laughs or giggles, voices, or a full range of human tones. This also may involve the speaking of isolated words.

While most hauntings refer to haunted locations, poltergeists have also been described as "haunted people". The "haunted" person would then be called the "agent" or "trigger". This term describes the one who is affected the most by the poltergeist activity, or the one that is most often present when activity takes place. With the exception of rare lengthy cases, poltergeist phenomena generally last from two to six weeks.

Some other typical phenomena may include but are not limited to the following:

- Constant pelting of your home with small rocks and stones.
- Objects or furniture being rolled, moved, overturned, otherwise agitated or levitated.
- The arrangement or neat stacking of objects into patterns.
- Bedclothes, linen, garments and curtains ripped, or otherwise damaged.
- Object(s) disappearing from their original location, and possibly turning up in an odd place.
- Object(s) seemingly appearing from nowhere.

- Electrical objects or appliances acting strangely such as turning on and off by themselves, even if they are not plugged in to an outlet.
- Telephones may ring or register calls.
- Mysterious pools of water and/or other liquids such as blood may appear to be emitted from normally dry surfaces.

Possession (Demonic)

Demonic possession is the complete takeover of a person's life, actions, personality, and body. Its major impact upon a person is physical, mental, emotional, and spiritual. It is a known fact that demons can also manipulate and inhabit animals, objects, and places. It is also thought that any place or situation that is relative to time and space can also come under the influence of demonic forces.

Residual Haunting

This is a location that has a spirit that does not interact with an individual that lives, works, or is passing through a location.

Scientific Method

The scientific method is a systematic means of exploring and explaining the world around us. Experiments are an important part of the scientific method.

The scientific method can be stated in a few different ways, however, it involves looking at the world around you, coming up with an explanation for what you observe, testing your explanation to see if it could be valid, and then either accepting your explanation or rejecting the explanation and trying to formulate a better one. Keep in mind that you must retain the integrity of all information accumulated.

Steps of the Scientific Method

1. Make an observation.
2. Ask a question.
3. Formulate a hypothesis.
4. Conduct an experiment.
5. Analyze your data and determine if you must accept or reject the hypothesis.
6. If you reject your hypothesis, you must return to step 3.

Spiritual Cleansing

A spiritual cleansing is a religious ceremony that calls upon a higher power to accomplish a spiritual cleaning and sealing of a person, place, and situation. It is also thought of as an act of faith upon the part of all participants. It can be called a house blessing or house exorcism. It can include the religious act of asking a higher power to bless or seal (sanctify) a person, place, animal, object, or situation.

Supernatural

Supernatural may at times refer to things that are beyond paranormal and may be attributed to higher beings such as angels, demons, etc

Voice Phenomenon

Direct Voice Phenomenon (DVP)- Have you ever thought you heard your name and no one is there? That is called Direct Voice Phenomenon (DVP). It is an auditory voice that comes from no discernible location or person.

Electronic Voice Phenomenon (EVP)- During paranormal investigations we walk around and ask the potential spirits questions.

You know that you did not hear anything yet when you replay the audio, you hear a distinct voice on the recording. This is known as Electronic Voice Phenomenon (EVP). The practice of asking potential spirits questions is known as EVP sessions or vigils. It is said that a spirit imprints a message on your recording device and you never heard it at the time when it happened.

Vortex

A vortex is considered to be a portal where a spirit may use to travel between our world and some other plane of existence. A vortex may also be a hole in time and space. Some consider vortices are more prominent on Ley Lines and this is a reason that one location may seem more active than other locations.

Resources

Carolina Society for Paranormal Research and Investigation Inc
(CSPRI Inc)

www.carolinaspri.net

American Institute for Paranormal Research

www.americaninstituteforparanormalresearch.net

The Paranormal Monitor

http://theparanormalmonitor.wordpress.com/

The Paranormal Exchange

http://theparanormalexchange.blogspot.com/

Paralina Radio Show

www.paralinaradio.com

The Holy Bible (King James Version)

Brandon's Email: brandon.hudgens@carolinaspri.net

Dennis' Email: dennis.carroll@carolinaspri.net

Made in the USA
Charleston, SC
30 October 2013